JIM MATHER
OF THE SUNDAY MIRROR
Solves Your Garden Problems

JIM MATHER
OF THE SUNDAY MIRROR

Solves Your Garden Problems

W. FOULSHAM & CO LTD
LONDON
NEW YORK
TORONTO
SYDNEY
CAPE TOWN

W. Foulsham & Company Ltd.
Yeovil Road, SLOUGH, Berkshire SL1 4JH

ISBN 0-572-01120-2
© W. Foulsham & Co. Ltd. (1981)

Photoset in Great Britain by
Rowland Phototypesetting Ltd, Bury St Edmunds, Suffolk
Printed by St Edmundsbury Press, Bury St Edmunds, Suffolk

Contents

TO MY FRIEND MARION WHO COMPILED
THE STIMULATING QUESTIONS
AND TO MY WIFE BILLIE
WHO HELPED WITH THE ANSWERS

Introduction

AS soon as we start gardening, we are liable to run into problems; small problems perhaps but difficult to sort out without experience, except by a long process of trial and error. In theory, gardening manuals tell us all we want to know about cultivation, but in practice they leave us guessing and asking questions.

Why so? It is not the fault of the manuals. If you consult a good medical dictionary you will find how to identify every human ailment and how to get the right treatment. But in practice you will be left guessing, because the diagnosis is so difficult. The medical book just cannot take the place of the doctor and nurse. Similarly, the gardening book does not take the place of the experienced gardener.

Under what heading in the manual are we to look when a healthy flowering plant fails to produce a flower? The failure may have no connection with any pest or disease. Plants behave in strange ways and guessing rarely produces a convincing explanation – or a remedy. In the end, we seek advice from an experienced gardener.

For many years I have been on the receiving end, listening to people's gardening worries and answering their questions. Hence, the publishers invited me to write this book as a question-and-answer exercise. From a long list of questions they submitted to me, I selected those which in my experience touch on popular matters in home gardening. I hope the book will make easy reading and that you will pick it up at odd moments to absorb snippets of useful information.

I advise you to try to avoid the problems rather than attempt to specialise in identifying them and treating them. Treatment, especially where it involves the use of chemicals, can be very expensive. Clean, tidy cultivation coupled with loving care, can do a great deal towards keeping your plants healthy, happy and disease-free. It can also reduce pest problems though we cannot avoid those marauding pests which come in over the fence. Many troubles are harboured in litter, debris and weeds. So if you keep the weeds down and clear away all rubbish and dead plants, you will have the basis of a trouble-free garden.

Chapter One

The Flower Garden

1

WHICH sex of tree carries the berries, male or female? I always understood that in trees, as in other vegetation, the female produced the seeds (which are in the berries) and yet I have seen a variety of holly called Golden King producing berries. I also understand that Golden Queen does NOT carry berries.

This is not a freak of nature but a bit of man's folly. It certainly is the female that carries the berries where plants are single-sexed. And this rule applies in hollies as in other subjects. But whoever named the holly varieties mentioned got the genders confused, for Golden King is the name of a FEMALE holly, and Golden Queen is the name of a MALE. There is another male called Silver Queen.

2

WHEN is it safe to saw the head out of a Lawson's Cypress, planted as a hedge, which has grown to 12 feet, with the aim of establishing a six-foot hedge?

It is safe almost any time provided you don't rest the ladder on the bit you are cutting off! But the safest time, for the good of the trees, is probably spring, just as new growth starts. Treat cuts with tree paint or lead paint.

3

WHAT is the botanical name of the true shamrock?

There isn't one, unless you have kissed the Blarney stone. Perhaps there is something in the fact that the name is half sham! But shamrock is what is termed in horticulture a "popular" name. It is not a botanical name and its use is not restricted to one species. In Ireland, if you are offered 'genuine' shamrock it will most likely be white clover. In England, it is more likely to be wood sorrel. Other shamrocks include yellow clover and black medick. But all shamrock is lovely and you should wear some on March 17th – St. Patrick's Day.

4

WHAT has caused my Sweet Violets to revert and produce white flowers instead of the popular violet-blue?

The term 'reversion' is frequently misused concerning plants whose characteristics appear to have changed. In this case, the plants have not reverted and indeed have not changed. What you are seeing are some self-sown seedlings which have popped up among your original plantings. If they spoil the effect, you can pull out the offending plants as soon as you see the colour of their blooms.

5

HOW can I keep sparrows off my polyanthus primroses (which these birds simply ruin) without doing any harm to my feathered friends?

There are deterrents which will work if applied frequently enough – they tend to wear off and wash off – but it might pay to find out why the birds peck the flowers. Almost certainly the birds are after insects and not the flowers themselves, so it is worth checking carefully for aphids and caterpillars. Getting rid of these, with a spray such as fenitrothion could eliminate what is attracting the birds.

6

WHAT is the reason people advocate putting plastic bags over pots of cuttings, bearing in mind that this can cause condensation which may set up rots and kill the cuttings?

The plastic bag or similar near-airtight device is to help soft-wood cuttings retain moisture until they form a root system which will provide new moisture supplies. The damp atmosphere achieves this and ensures that the cutting makes roots before it collapses. But this damp atmosphere is not intended to be kept up long enough to encourage moulds and rots. The aim is quick rooting, because soft cuttings must root quickly or die anyway. Incidentally, the atmosphere inside the plastic covering should not be stagnant. Either the inside of the bag must be wiped every day or there should be air-holes.

7

WHEN a cool greenhouse is used to raise boxes of flowering plants to plant out, why do the seedlings get too tall and spindly?

In dull weather, the seedlings reach vainly for the sun and so grow leggy. The way to avoid this is to rig up temporary shelving to put the boxes up to as near the greenhouse roof as possible.

8

WHY do some geraniums grow long spindly stems while others make dense, bushy growth with lots of stems and lots of flowers?

It is simply a matter of training. Left alone, a young geranium will tend not to make large numbers of side-shoots. But if the growing tip is pinched out, then two (sometimes three) shoots will grow to replace the one pinched out. So the drill is to pinch out the tip of the initial stem when it is only three or four inches tall and then to pinch out the tips of the new shoots when they have made a little growth. The more pinching out the more bushy the plant, but don't overdo it.

9

HOW should one plant paeonies so that they do not fail to bloom? They seem to stop blooming after transplanting.

Paeonies prefer to be planted in early autumn rather than spring, and they like the shallowest possible planting. They are sulky characters and do not like being disturbed. Hence their refusal to bloom after being moved. How long they take to get over it is unpredictable but the best that can be done is to try to ensure that they are moved at the right time and with the minimum of root disturbance.

10

WHY are paeonies such a failure as cut flowers? The flowers look lovely when freshly cut but their petals fall off after only one day.

I don't know why they behave like that, but it can be corrected. The remedy is to cut them just as they start to open and lay them flat in a cold room for 24 hours. Then snip an inch off each stem before putting them in deep vases of water. The flowers so treated will have a normal vase life without dropping their petals.

11

HOW does one recognise bacterial canker in an ornamental cherry? Some shoots have died off and there are festering wounds. Are these the symptoms and is there a cure?

The description certainly fits bacterial canker. Spray thoroughly with Bordeaux mixture three times at three-week intervals. Dead wood should be cut out promptly but general pruning should be done in mid-summer. All cuts and wounds should be treated with canker paint.

12

WHEN is the best time to split a clump of Pampas Grass which has grown too big?

April is the time to do it but first you should set fire to the clump in February to burn the leaves because they can cut like razors and make handling a hazardous job. Then dig it up in April, split up the roots and replant each piece immediately.

13

HOW does one dry Pampas Grass plumes for indoor decoration?

The plumes are best cut just as they are opening. But even after they have opened fully I have brought them in, without treatment, and they kept perfectly.

14

WHAT sort of dye should be used to colour the plumes of Pampas Grass?

Paint makes a better job than can be done with dyes. Fasten each plume to a stake in an outside spot sheltered from the wind and spray it with an aerosol of car paint. The weather must be calm.

15

WHAT sort of soil is best for heathers?

Generally a rather poor, sandy and slightly acid soil is well suited for heather but such soil should be improved by the addition of moist peat in each planting hole so that the plants can get going quickly. Overhead watering is needed in dry weather till the roots are established.

16

WHY do those colourful Russell lupins die or revert to common blue?

There are various possible reasons why they die and they are certainly not long lived, but they do not revert. The blue-flowered plants are self-sown seedlings which spring up from seed dropped by the Russells. When lupins seed themselves, the strongest seedlings choke out the others, and the strongest are usually the blue-flowered ones. Fresh plants should be raised from seed every three or four years if you want to maintain a good show of Russell lupins.

17

WHAT causes brown erratic wavy lines on chrysanthemum leaves? Spraying with fungicides and insecticides does not seem to touch it and it keeps spreading to new leaves.

The trouble is a leaf miner grub which tunnels inside the leaves. Spraying with HCH (formerly called BHC) is normally effective but two or three sprays may be needed.

18

WHAT should be done about blobs of froth which appear on some of the plants in my border? I am told that this is cuckoo's spit. Is it harmful and if so what should be done?

This is a pest. It is known as Cuckoo Spit but has nothing to do with cuckoos. It is the larva of the froghopper, which sucks the plant sap, and surrounds itself with the froth as a protection. A systemic insecticide ought to be effective but if spraying is done forcefully enough with any good insecticide the froth can be blown aside to allow the chemical to reach the pest.

19

WHAT chances are there of keeping a fuchsia of doubtful hardiness outdoors during the winter? Would it survive if covered with a plastic bag?

Possibly, but condensation could create problems. If no protection (such as greenhouse or frame) is available, I should just leave it out and cover the bottom six inches of stems with light soil. That should be enough to keep frost from the base of the stems and the roots, if enough soil is used in this earthing up. Remove the soil in late spring after the frosts have finished and trim the stems down to the point where fresh growth is seen. The old stems will die down to ground level but don't discard the plant just because it looks dead. Give it time.

20

WHEN is the best time to plant out dahlias? Some say early May and some say not before frosts have finished.

Green plants, grown from cuttings must not be planted out till spring frosts have finished in say late May or early June. But dahlias are also planted as tubers which would not be sending up shoots immediately after planting. So these are normally planted in late April or early May.

21

WILL dahlias grow satisfactorily from cut-up pieces of large tubers as is sometimes done with large seed potatoes?

No. Roots can be split up (carefully pulled apart) provided each piece has a stem. Dahlia roots are not true tubers like potatoes. Pieces without stems will not sprout because they have no "eyes" like potatoes have. The new shoots spring from the base of the old stem.

22

WHEN dahlias roots are dug up for storing at the end of the season, how short should the stems be cut?

Cut them down to about six inches, rub the soil off the roots (DON'T wash them) and stand them upside down in a frost-proof place to drain hollow stems before storing.

23

WHEN is the correct time for outdoor planting of daffodil and tulip bulbs?

The term 'correct' is rather too precise. Daffodils like to make roots while the soil is warm, so they should be planted in September – or early as possible. On the other hand, tulips may make early shoots, which could be hit by frost, if planted early, and so they are best held back till November. But when all has been said, the bulbs are all pretty accommodating and as often as not are planted at the same time – October, November or December. It is more important that the soil should be good and well drained.

24

WHY do some gardeners tie up daffodil leaves after the flowers fade? and is it a good practice?

It is done to keep them tidy and (on lawns) to make it easier to mow around them. It does no good, and restricts the breathing of the leaves. It is much better for the leaves to be left to die off naturally. For tidiness, they can be cut down when the top two inches of the leaves have gone brown, but they must not be cut down earlier or the bulbs will not have finished preparing for the following year's flowers.

25

WILL daffodils bloom better if left in the ground permanently? I have had some blooming for two years but the next year there were no flowers. So this year I discarded them. Incidentally, I always dig them up after flowering.

They do better if left undisturbed but I think you were too hasty in discarding them. They would have recovered. Barring pest or disease damage, the blindness indicates that they were lifted too soon, before the leaves had died down naturally to indicate that the bulb had completed its season's work and would be ready to bloom again after a rest.

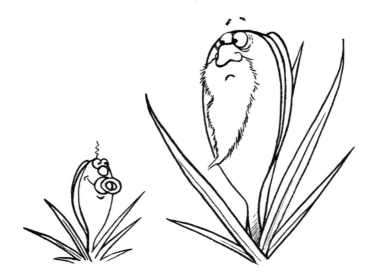

26

HOW true is it that crocus corms live only one year? I heard that a new corm grows above the old each year and the old one dies, but if that were so the corms would soon come to the surface.

It is quite true that the old corm dies and a new one grows immediately above it. But the new corm makes what are called "contractile roots" which pull it down to the correct depth.

27

WILL freesia corms planted outdoors survive the winter or is it better to dig them up and store them?

Freesias which flower outdoors are specially "prepared" corms, and they flower out of season. They will not repeat the performance, so you should dig them up and treat them in future as indoor flowers; that is, plant them in pots during autumn.

28

WHAT is the proper name of autumn-flowering plants which look like crocuses and are known as Naked Ladies? When is the time to plant them?

They are Colchicum autumnale and are grown from corms planted in summer. They look good in a lawn. Leaf growth (without flowers) appears in spring and should not be cut till the leaves die down in July.

29

WHY is it that hyacinth bulbs grown in bowls of fibre are useless after flowering while those grown in soil will flower again?

There is not sufficient nourishment in the fibre to feed up the bulb. Fibre is used in bowls as a matter of convenience because it stays sweet without drainage whereas soil would go sour in like circumstances. But it is not right to say that bulbs are 'useless' after a season in fibre. They are just temporarily exhausted, and after a season in the soil they will pick up. So they should be planted in a spare corner in the garden and not thrown away.

30

WHY should bulbs of Fritillaria Crown Imperial fail repeatedly when planted eight inches deep, in October, in well-drained soil?

One can never be certain what causes failure but bulbs planted at that depth in a wet winter could suffer from water settling in the centre of the bulb. This could cause decay. To avoid this, plant the bulbs ON THEIR SIDES. They will right themselves.

31

WHAT situation and what soil depth is best for Golden Clarion lilies? Mine in full sun have done poorly. I wondered whether they needed shade but it is suggested that perhaps they ought to be planted deeper since they root on their stems.

It is true that they prefer to be planted deep enough to encourage stem rooting but the fact is that if they are planted near the surface they grow special roots to pull themselves down deeper. You are right about the need for shade on the soil, though the stems enjoy the sun. Use a few dwarf bedding plants to shade the roots.

32

WILL snowdrops recover if transplanted in full bloom and if the plants seem immediately to have died?

Snowdrops are not easy to re-establish so there is always a risk. But the BEST time to transplant them is when they are in flower. Even though the leaves die off, there is a chance they will pick up and flower the following January

33

WHAT is the name of the double snowdrop and is it related to the common snowdrop?

It is simply a double form of the common snowdrop, and its name is Galanthus nivalis flore pleno. Cultivation is exactly the same, which means it can be raised from seeds, taking about five years to reach the flowering stage; or bulbs can be planted. The bulbs flower in the spring following autumn planting.

34

WHAT is the difference, if any, between the Guernsey Lily and the Jersey Lily?

The Jersey Lily is Amaryllis belladonna, which has much bigger blooms than the Guernsey Lily (Merine sarniensis). They are both bulbs and they flower in autumn.

35

WILL perennial phlox flower better if watering is always done only at night-time?

It sounds suspiciously like "shepherds watch their phlox by night". However there is sense in the idea. Phlox quickly droop if the roots go dry, so must be well watered in dry weather. And evening is a good time to water because the moisture can reach the roots and not evaporate in the sun. But I should not take it too seriously; water when it is convenient and use a mulch to slow-down the drying.

36

WHAT causes whole batches of asters to collapse when only about three inches high, even when the seed has been sown in good composts and the seedlings planted out with care?

The trouble is Aster Wilt fungus, which lives for years in the soil. There are wilt resistant varieties, but even with them it is best to plant where asters have not been grown before, and so avoid the risk of infection.

37

WILL sunflowers ripen up their seeds enough to justify growing them to provide oil for cooking?

In an average summer the seed should be good enough. But the problem would be squeezing the sunflower seeds. It is like trying to get blood from stones. A strong mechanical crusher would be needed to crush oil from such hard seeds.

38

WHEN is the time to divide a root of incarvillea – the pretty border plant with fernlike leaves and pink trumpet flowers?

September or October is the right time but splitting the root is very difficult. You will need a strong, sharp tool like a butcher's cleaver, or a large carving knife and a heavy mallet.

39

HOW can one cope with insects in a garden pool? The leaves of water lilies have been badly damaged by midges, but as there are fish in the pool an insecticide would be dangerous.

The answer is to lift out the plants and soak them in derris for an hour. They must then be washed thoroughly, after which it will be safe to put them back into the pool. But if there were enough golden orfe in the pool, these fish would eat all the midges.

40

WHEN biennial flowers are raised from seed in the greenhouse for planting out, how long should be devoted to hardening them off? And what is the method?

Allow about three weeks, but it varies according to weather. Since the change must be gradual, the time needed depends on the size of the gap to be bridged — the difference between indoor and outdoor temperatures. Transfer the plants from the greenhouse to a cold frame and raise the glass lid a little more each day during daylight hours till it can be removed entirely, except at night. After that, increase ventilation each night (barring frost) till night protection too can be discarded.

41

HOW does one train a new beech hedge to make it bushy? Is it correct that the hedge must not be cut till it reaches the desired height?

Early topping will not make it bushy as it would with privet. But some light trimming can be done from the start. You can reduce every shoot by a quarter every year till the desired shape and height are reached. Do it in August if you want the leaves to stay on all winter.

42

WHEN starting a new garden, where the aim is to establish a hedge rapidly, would Leyland Cypress be the ideal choice?

Not ideal, unless it is a very large garden needing a very tall hedge. The faster a hedge grows, the sooner it gets too big. Leyland Cypress is good for a hedge about 15 feet tall, but for the average garden, Lawson's Cypress is more manageable. It is not too slow and can be kept down reasonably to a height of six or seven feet.

43

HOW can one restore a privet hedge which has gone scraggy with very little leaf? Can it be cut down to about one foot tall, and will it then re-grow as a bushy hedge?

The severe cutting back should do the trick if it is properly timed. Do it in late April or early May, when the season's new growth is beginning. Do not attempt it in autumn or winter, because hard cutting at that time is liable to cause severe die-back in privet.

44

WHAT is the difference between quickthorn and hawthorn?

Quickthorn is just another name for the common hawthorn, especially when it is being used for hedging.

45

WHAT is the Silver Leaf disease, which attacks a privet hedge? Is it the same as attacks plum trees? The privet leaves are only slightly silvered, and are crinkly. The whole hedge is sickly.

This is not the Silver Leaf fungus at all. The trouble is caused by thrips, which are sucking insects. Spray the hedge with fenitrothion and repeat after three weeks if new growth is not clean. As soon as the pests are cleared, the silvering effect will disappear.

46

WHEN planting a hedge of common holly, which will take about 20 plants, must male and female be planted alternatively all the way along if I want berries?

No. Three males would be quite enough, as one male will pollinate six or seven females.

47

HOW soon can a privet hedge be replaced after the first has died of Honey Fungus? The old hedge was put on the bonfire and the site cleared and dug.

The fungus can linger for years and it would be better not to plant privet. Lonicera nitida is somewhat similar to privet but has some resistance to Honey Fungus. Whatever is to be planted, every scrap of old root must be dug out and the soil should be treated with formaldehyde two months before the new hedge is planted.

48

WHAT is the name of the Christmas tree, and when is the best time to plant one? Can it be planted out after use indoors?

Norway spruce (Picea abies) can be planted in winter whenever the ground is workable. If it is transplanted into a tub of soil, to bring indoors as a Christmas tree, care should be taken not to let it dry out. The indoor atmosphere over the Yuletide holiday tends to be too warm and dry but there is a plastic spray (called simply S 600) which can be applied immediately before the tree is brought in. This seals the needles and helps to prevent drying out.

49

WILL mistletoe grow from berries stuck on an old apple tree?

Possibly. The drill is to squash the berries into the rough bark on the undersides of branches. This should be done in February but it is a double gamble because not all mistletoes live on apple and your seeds will need to produce both male and female plants if you are to get berries. Even then, the plants will probably take about seven years to reach maturity and start berrying. Other hosts from which your sprig of mistletoe may have come are Ash, Hawthorn, Lime, Poplar, Maple, Mountain Ash and Oak. And, of course, the seed would do best on the host from which the sprig came.

50

WHERE a climbing plant, Virginia Creeper, has been planted too far away from the wall instead of close in, and is going everywhere except on to the wall, when is the best time to replant it closer in?

If it is not more than two feet from the wall, do NOT replant it. Lead a strong shoot along the ground and on to the wall, using a short stick to help train it. As soon as it touches the wall it will cling and climb. It is a mistake to put the roots close up to the wall, because the wall acts like blotting paper and draws moisture up from the soil. If you are sure yours is too far from the wall, replant in autumn.

51

WHEN the blossoms on a young camellia go brown, presumably due to morning sun after frost, would the plant be better moved to a west-facing wall away from the early sun? If so, when is the best time to move it?

It would certainly be better beside a west wall because although the blossoms like sun they don't want it while they are frosted. The sudden thawing damages the petals. Move it in April or September. Handle the roots with care as they are easily damaged.

52

HOW does one get rid of woodworm in a lilac tree? Some of the shoots have been tunnelled by this timber pest and severely damaged.

This is not the common timber woodworm, but the larva of the Wood Leopard Moth, a fruit pest which uses lilac as a host plant. The only effective treatment is to cut off and burn all bored shoots.

53

WHY do blackbirds strip the lovely red berries off firethorn (pyracantha) and leave the yellow-berried variety alone?

Probably red attracts them more, and although the yellow firethorn seems to be left alone while the red is ravaged the birds are quite likely to turn to that later. And blackbirds are not the only culprits. You can use a deterrent spray to make the berries taste unpleasant and reduce the damage without harming the birds.

54

WHICH species of ivy has oval leaves, no clingers, and black berries?

This is a fair description of the common ivy and not of a rare species. Mature, fertile shoots of ivy are like that. They lose the traditional ivy character, but they are no freak. The ivy climbs by producing aerial roots with which it clings to walls or trees. As long as it is producing these aerial roots it does not mature and make berries. But when it reaches the top of its support and ceases to climb it changes the shape of its leaf and begins to fruit.

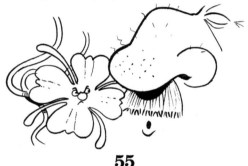

55

WHY does honeysuckle sometimes seem to have no scent even when it grows and blooms well? Is this due to the soil or is the plant exhausted?

Neither. Honeysuckle likes a moist soil and although it thrives in bright weather, its scent in those conditions is not strong. In the evening shade, or just after a shower, the scent is inescapable. The lips should be kept OPEN while sniffing any scented blossom if the full fragrance is to be enjoyed.

56

WHEN is the best time to prune Weigela (or Diervilla florida) to get the maximum show of bloom?

This shrub, with flowers like foxgloves, blooms in May/June and should be pruned immediately after blooming. Either a few of the old stems can be cut down to ground level, or every shoot can be cut back to a point from which new growth is springing.

57

WHEN azaleas are doing badly because of poor, chalky soil, is it possible to plant them in tubs of lime-free compost? Can one make such a compost?

You can make a lime-free compost with three parts peat and one part sand, plus normal nutrients and excluding the lime (chalk) that is a standard additive to John Innes composts. But the whole operation may be unnecessary. Sequestrenes applied to the soil at rates prescribed on the pack could be used to correct the soil where the plants are now growing.

58

WHEN wisteria has been planted four years against a sunny wall and is making lots of leaf, but no bloom, what treatment does it want?

Wisteria can be slow. Cut back all new shoots to six or eight inches in July/August each year if it is making excessive leaf and shoot growth but no blooms. When growth and flowering settle down to a normal pattern, you can prune in February, cutting the season's young growth back to five or six buds.

59

WHY should a healthy-looking clematis with the roots in the shade and well watered, fail to swell its buds? Why do stems die too?

This sounds like clematis wilt, which is a baffling problem, but often the plant gets over the trouble. Cut down the dead stems, and pray for new growth. Spraying with Benlate in spring and early summer will help to prevent attacks.

60

HOW should one treat a climber called Dutchman's Pipe planted more than a year against a warm wall, which has made only one straight, tall stem. Is there any way to make it spread?

Dutchman's Pipe (Aristolochia) tends to do this, unless the growing tip is pinched out (preferably in May). New shoots which spring out after the pinching back, should be trained out sideways.

61

WHEN a passion flower planted outside and trained over a doorway makes vigorous growth but no flowers, would it help to plant it in a tub to control its roots?

Perhaps that would curb its passion but the roots would be better left alone. During the winter, cut back all side-shoots to about six inches and cut overcrowding surplus stems down to ground level.

62

WHAT is the best way to prune a shrub called forsythia which at present is growing well? The yellow flowers are very attractive and the aim is to maintain them.

As soon as the flowers have fallen, it is essential to cut back each stem that has flowered. Cut right down to a good new growth bud. At the same time, reduce crowding by cutting a few old stems down to ground level. The blooms grow on the young wood which grows during summer and autumn after the pruning.

63

WHAT can be done with rose bushes that have become too tall with bare, black stems? My gardening book says: "only in exceptional cases should you cut into wood more than a year old". By following that advice I have let mine get too tall.

Cut down one old stem each year on each bush, to within four inches of the ground to encourage new low shoots. Or, if the bush has more than three stems cut two of them down in the first year. In future do not take the term "only in exceptional cases" too literally. Certainly if all the stems were allowed to get tall and woody it would be bad to cut them all right down but it is wise not to let all the stems grow old. Always have at least one young shoot growing from near the base.

64

WHAT causes leaves of my roses to turn from shiny green to dull bronze? Some also have fine threads similar to spiders' webs. Any connection. I can see no spiders.

The tiny Red Spider spins a delicate web. It is the mite of this spider that sucks the sap and causes the bronzing. So there is a definite connection. The tiny red spiders are there, so you can see their fine webs; while the spider-mites, which do the damage to the plants, are sucking at the leaves. Spray thoroughly with a systemic insecticide and repeat as necessary. If you use a magnifying glass you will find the pests.

65

WHEN a garden is being re-planned and roses have to be moved from one side of the garden to the other, is it necessary to wait till the leaves fall, and do the job in bleak winter weather?

In theory, yes. Lifting a plant in full leaf gives it a shock. But the shock is insignificant when the growing season is over, say in late October. So the transplanting can be done then instead of waiting and having to work in uncomfortable conditions.

66

WHEN I received a large package of rose bushes as a Christmas gift they arrived with instructions that they must be heeled in till the ground was right for planting. What does "heeled in" mean and what is its significance?

Heeling-in is temporary planting so that the plants do not dry out while they wait for the ground to be ready for permanent planting. Make a shallow trench; set the plants in at an angle, and heap soil over the roots and the lower part of the stems. Planting at an angle helps reduce sap flow. The object of the exercise is to cope with the fact that ground may not be in a suitable condition (too wet for instance) at the time the plants arrive, especially when they are not expected. Care should be taken not to damage the labels by burying them.

67

WHAT causes the leaves of my rose bushes to go like a Zebra Plant – all striped – with the veins green, and between the veins yellow?

Thin stripes of green indicate iron shortage and should be treated with sequestrene. If the green and yellow stripes are equal in width, magnesium is more likely to be the need. Give epsom salts at 1 oz to 1 sq. yard. But better still: do a soil test.

68

WHY do some people advise taking nine-inch cuttings of mature rose stems in October and planting them six inches deep in the open garden, while expert growers all propagate by grafting?

Commercial growers propagate roses by 'budding' which is a form of grafting, because that method is much more productive. There will be six or more good "eyes" (growth buds) on each piece of shoot used as a cutting. Thus, by budding the grower can get that number of plants instead of one. This does not matter to the domestic grower, whose garden will provide more cuttings than he needs, but it is important to the commercial grower, especially in the early days of a new variety when the number of plants is limited. One important bonus you get when you raise roses from cuttings is that you get no 'suckers', those unwanted shoots which grow up from the rootstocks of budded plants. By the way, labour costs being high and skills being scarce, commercial growers are no longer certain that budding is clearly superior to rooting cuttings.

69

HOW is it that rose mildew continues to spread AFTER plants have been sprayed with a systemic fungicide? It is appreciated that mildew sprays are preventive, and will not help much on infected shoots, but why does not the systemic spray act as a preventive and protect the new young shoots which grow out after spraying?

Once mildew gets in, there is a battle between the fungus and the chemical, and a fortnightly spray with a systemic fungicide may do no more than check. It is worst on moist, sheltered sites. Remove and burn infected shoots in winter; start spraying before the next spring growth begins. If you then do fortnightly spraying, control should be complete.

70

WHAT causes rose buds to fail to swell and to go brown and fail to open? Also the stems seem to get mildew and die off.

This is a fungal disease called botrytis and calls for preventive treatment. Spraying with thiram or zineb while the buds are just forming should keep it off. But if the trouble gets in, cut off and burn infected shoots.

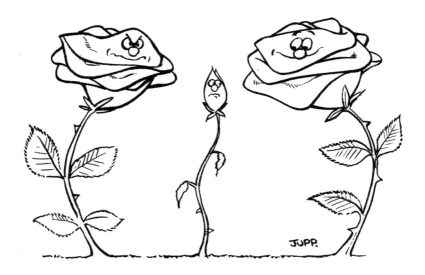

71

WHY do buds on some roses swell to full fat size and then go brown and rot instead of opening? And what is the best way to cope with it?

This trouble is called 'balling' and is not a disease. Wet weather causes outer petals to cling together. If you peel them off in time, before several layers of petals are blighted, the bud should open. Anyway, the trouble passes as the weather turns drier.

72

WHEN is the best time to spread a mulch of peat or leaf mould on a rose-bed to cope with water shortage? And how much should be used?

Timing depends on the weather. This sort of mulch should not be put on to dust-dry soil. The soil, and the leafmould, should both be moist, otherwise the mulch will help to keep the roots dry instead of moist. Nor should it be put on too early before the soil has warmed up. So wait till the soil has warmed up – but not dried out – in late spring.

73

WHEN planting climbing roses against a tall boundary fence does it matter if the fence gets no sun? Surely, although the sun shines on the other side of the fence, the shady side of the fence will get warm from behind.

There is not much choice if it is a boundary fence, but while the roses will grow up the fence, most of the blooms on a climber will tend to appear at the top and turn their faces to the sun (over the fence). So the neighbours get the beauty of them. Your aim on a shady fence must be to keep the growth trained fanwise or horizontal and not to encourage any shoots to go above the height of the fence.

74

WHAT causes healthy roses to revert and produce wild blooms like we see in the hedgerows?

Roses which do this have not reverted: the grafted variety has just died. Sucker shoots have grown from the roots and starved the cultivated variety. Royal National Rose Society tests suggests that roses grown on a rootstock called Laxa are the least likely to behave like this.

75

WHAT must be done to a sandy soil to make it suitable for roses?

Much the same as for most garden shrubs and trees. A soil that is too light and sandy will not hold adequate reserves of nutrients or moisture because it drains too freely. Hence, the answer is to enrich it with spongy material such as peat and leaf mould. But if the suggestion is that roses need clay, then it is an exaggeration. Many roses are grown on rootstocks of Rosa Canina (the Dog Rose) which enjoys a clay soil (not plain clay) but does not demand it. Almost any soil, properly cultivated, will accommodate roses, but they are very unhappy on chalky ground.

76

WILL any specific form of pruning help a rose called Climbing Masquerade to produce flowers? The rose grows vigorously and is healthy and has been pruned to keep it from going too high, but has not been pruned excessively. Yet it does not bloom.

Roses whose names are prefixed by 'Climbing' will presumably be climbing 'sports' of bush types such as floribundas and hybrid-teas. They have 'sported', which botanically indicates a mutation or change of character. But they retain one former characteristic, namely that of carrying most of their flowers towards the tips of their shoots. Hence you must either let them go up and produce their blooms above your head, or you must train them sideways and hope that upward-growing side-shoots will bloom before going sky-high. So the answer is, yes, the right pruning will help, but that means the minimum of trimming while training the stems to grow as near the horizontal as possible.

77

WHAT causes approved garden spray chemicals to damage rose leaves? As soon as the weather gets hot I know roses need a spray for Black Spot, but when sprayed they promptly develop brown spots; obviously a result of the spraying. Is it because the spray is too strong or does it want a fine mister?

Mister who? The most likely cause is spraying in strong sunshine, which produces scorch spots even with a fine-mist spray. The chemical must dry naturally, out of direct sun, so time the spraying for when the sun is off the plants.

78

WHY is preventive spraying, even with a systemic insecticide so ineffective against greenfly? Even when plants are sprayed early, the first emerging leaves seem still to have greenfly.

Systemic insecticides have to be absorbed by the plant, and leafless plants cannot absorb much spray so that type of insecticide is not much use before leaves open. But whatever insecticide is used (as distinct from winter spraying with chemicals to kill eggs) it is better to wait and watch for the pests to start hatching out, rather than spray too soon.

79

HOW is one expected to keep flowers healthy when one is advised not to spray plants in bloom, although pests are active all through the blooming season?

You must not spray open blooms or you will kill bees and damage the blooms. You can direct a systemic insecticide on to the leaves and it will work through the plant, without damaging the blooms. Preferably, spray at dusk when bees have gone to their hives and settled down for the night.

80

WHEN my flowerbeds were awfully weedy it was suggested that the weeds had come from lawn mowings I put on. But, having overcome this problem with lawn weedkiller, I am now advised that the mowings would poison the plants. So what does one do?

It is not good to use fresh mowings as a mulch anyway, whether or not they are full of weed seeds. Nor should you use mowings from lawns treated with hormone weedkiller. It is much better to put the mowings on the compost heap and allow at least six months before using the compost.

81

WHAT hope is there for a Monkey Puzzle tree which looks healthy but does not seem to grow? It is about 18 years old, and was moved after 12 years because it was only four feet tall then. It is still struggling and not making much growth.

This tree (Araucaria), normally takes ten years or so to reach four feet tall, so it ought not to have been moved. It ought to grow about a foot a year after the first ten years or so but not after being disturbed. If you give the ground a mulch each spring and leave the tree undisturbed, it will soon be all right.

82

WHAT causes a large lavender bush to wilt and die one stem at a time? It must be something in the soil because when it was replaced by a young one, this one went the same way.

Yes indeed it is something in the soil. The trouble is a soil-borne fungus called Shab and it is useless to plant another lavender in the same spot because the fungus will keep on striking.

83

WHY does a palm tree, a Cordyline australis, suddenly die after flourishing for some years in a snug corner? There are many shoots coming from the base, so it is not completely dead.

It is hard to guess the precise trouble but most likely the winter was a bit too bitter for it. The new shoots referred to will be suckers which should be allowed to develop. They can be transplanted in April and the old plant should then be dug up and put on the bonfire.

84

WHAT can be done to help a Tulip Tree bought from a good nursery, which is some years old but has never shown any sign of flowering?

The Tulip Tree (Liriodendron tulipifera) is not likely to bloom till it is at least 15 years old, and even then the first flowers may be hard to see because they will be at the very top of the tree. But there is no special attention needed and nothing effective that can be done to speed the tree's maturity

Chapter Two

Vegetables

85

WHAT causes some of the first fruits of my tomatoes to have a circular black patch (rotting) on the side opposite the stalk?

This is Blossom End Rot and is due to irregular watering, especially when the weather is warm and the fruits are swelling. The cells at the blossom end of the fruit collapse and fail. Any damage such as this speeds the ripening of the affected fruit and that is why you find it on some of the first to colour up. Blossom End Rot is not a disease, but a physiological disorder.

86

WILL the peat compost in which tomatoes have been grown in pots in the greenhouse be suitable for potatoes? And can I use the same ten-inch pots for the potatoes?

Yes. If you plant the potatoes in January or February, using the previous year's compost, and harvest the potatoes small, the pots will be free in April/May in time for tomatoes. But remember you MUST use fresh, sterilized compost for the tomatoes.

87

What is the reason for transplanting tomatoes several times instead of once? And won't this disturb the roots? For instance I have some large pots and I am buying tomato plants in three-inch pots. Must I transplant first into five-inch pots before potting up into the large pots?

It is not absolutely essential, provided you transplant them low down in the ten-inch pot and add just an inch more compost at intervals of about a week till the pot is full. Fresh roots will grow on the stem and fill the pot. The vital thing is not to put a small root system into a large volume of soil in a pot. In open ground it is different – provided watering is restricted to the ball of soil in which roots are active.

88

WHEN greenhouse tomatoes grown in growing-bags are healthy and free from disease is there any reason why the bags should not be re-used? It seems an expensive waste.

Using them again for tomatoes brings a high risk of root infection, despite a year's clean record. But with nutrients added, the compost can be used again, for plants with less sensitive root systems.

89

WHY are we told not to start feeding tomato plants until the first truss of fruit has set?

Assuming that the plants are in the rich compost they need, the advice is sound. Feeding before fruits start setting, will encourage excess stem and leaf growth. Once fruit is set, it can make use of the extra nutrients. But it is important to give weak feeds and not over-strong doses. A weak feed twice a week is better than a very strong feed once a fortnight.

90

WHAT is the right stage at which to harvest tomatoes? Some people pick as soon as the fruits show yellow while some leave them to go red, and I know that big growers never leave them to ripen on the plants.

For the fullest flavour the fruit should ripen on the plant. On the other hand, if you pick the first ones half ripe, you help the plant swell its later fruits. Commercial growers must pick early to allow time for transit and to avoid the risk of putting over-ripe fruits into the shop. Take your pick!

91

WHEN the season is finished and the last of the tomatoes have to be picked green, is it wise to put them in a drawer to ripen? Does it help to wrap each one? And if so what wrapping is best?

Yes, they ripen reasonably in a drawer. Wrapped fruits are less likely to shrivel, and the wrapping also reduces the spread of rot. Waxed paper is the best material for wrapping, but old newspapers will do.

92

WHY do some of my Ailsa Craig tomatoes grown indoors have a hard green patch near the stalk when they ripen, despite shading from direct sun. I understood that this greening was caused by direct sun on the fruit.

"Greenback" as it is called can be due to sunscorch, or extra high temperatures, and even to shortage of potash. Use more potash, control temperature by good ventilation and try a variety which is less prone to this trouble – such as Craigella, which is a strain of Ailsa Craig.

93

WHAT causes the stems of tomato seedlings to rot at soil level and the seedlings to collapse? Some say it is dirty soil but what does that mean?

"Dirty" soil is that which harbours diseases, pests, weed seeds and harmful bacteria. It should be heat-treated to kill off these before being used in seed boxes. In dirty soil, a fungus disease called Damping Off can cause the sort of collapse referred to in the question.

94

WHAT makes tomato fruits split? I understood it was due to irregular watering but I take infinite care in my six feet by six feet greenhouse and they still split.

When they split, it suggests that the air is too dry or too hot, which is not surprising in a small structure in a hot summer. Keep the glass shaded, the floor wet, and fit extra ventilators – besides taking care over the watering. The smaller the greenhouse the more difficult it is to avoid extremes of temperature and moisture content.

95

WHEN growing tomatoes by "ring culture" in the greenhouse border does one feed and water the soil in the pots or put all fertilizers into the "aggregate" beneath the pots?

The pots and the aggregate want different treatments. The feeding roots of the plants are in the pots and that is where the plant food should go. But you must also soak beneath with plain water, when necessary to ensure that the tap roots do not go short of moisture.

96

WHY am I advised not to save seed from a tomato called Grenadier on the ground of its being an F1 hybrid? I am told that seed from any F1 hybrid is useless, but if that is so, how do seedsmen get good seed?

To produce hybrid seed, flowers of the chosen "mother" variety are emasculated and pollinated by the "father" variety, and this cross-pollination has to be done year after year. You can save seed from your fruit if you wish, and it will produce plants. But fruits from them would not be F1 and would not be Grenadier. Their quality would be unpredictable.

97

WHAT sort of pollination or cross-pollination is needed to get fruits from the peppers (capsicum) which I grow in seven-inch pots of a peat compost in my greenhouse. The flowers keep falling off and failing to set fruit.

A hot tip for your peppers is to syringe the plants daily with plain water in dry weather to help the flowers set their fruits. When fruits set, feed the plants weekly. Cross-pollination is not needed, and indeed the syringing should not be overdone or you may overload the plants.

98

WHAT is the difference between the large green pepper and the large red one? I want to grow some indoors but cannot make up my mind which to try.

They are the same fruit. We usually pick them green because they are slow to turn red, but in any event the flavour is just as good when they are green.

99

HOW many fruits should I allow on an Egg Plant (aubergine)? Do I have to stop it (nip out the growing tip) at some stage?

When four fruits have set on an aubergine most people nip off further blooms. From this stage, side shoots also are removed, excessive growth discouraged, and liquid feeds given. But given a good start and a good summer, you might get six or more, from each plant. It depends to some extent on how big you want each fruit to swell.

100

WHAT causes the fruits of Egg Plants to go mildewed and start to rot? Fruits seem to rot off at the stalk end.

Botrytis or Grey Mould, is an airborne fungus which attacks dying tissues, such as the flower petals, especially in cool, damp, conditions. Proper spraying can prevent but not cure it. Burn infected parts of plants, then spray, with a suitable fungicide, such as benomyl.

It helps a great deal if the fading petals of blooms are tugged off gently immediately the tiny fruit (less than pea-size) is seen. This removes the main source of trouble. Good ventilation also is important.

101

WHAT can be done to prevent parsnips from developing a nasty browning at the crown? I believe it is called parsnip canker.

The trouble does not normally afflict sound, undamaged roots, but gets into cracks, which may follow a dry spell, or into holes made by carrot rootfly maggots. Avoid the cracks by watering in dry weather to keep the plants growing strongly. Dust with bromophos to keep off rootfly.

102

WHY do parsnips sometimes make lots of little finger-like roots instead of a long, single, thick root?

This trouble is most likely to occur in lush, freshly-manured ground. Bulky manure should not be applied later than the autumn before the spring sowing. Granulated fertilizers at sowing time would not cause forking.

103

WHAT is the reason my carrot leaves turn yellow, then red, and collapse when the carrots are the size of a little finger? It has happened two successive years.

This sounds like Motley Dwarf Disease, which is caused by a virus. Since the virus lives in the soil, carrots should be grown as far as possible from the infected area in future. Diseased plants should be put on the bonfire.

104

WHY do some people say that frost improves the flavour of parsnips? And if there is any truth in it, why do growers dig up the roots and store them instead of leaving them at the mercy of the winter weather?

Frost helps convert more of the starch into sugar and so sweeten the parsnip and improve the flavour. It is wise to dig some and store them rather than risk having to dig ground as hard as concrete whenever you happen to fancy a few parsnips during a spell of severe frost.

105

WHY does my beetroot always go to seed? My neighbour's does the same. Is there any way of avoiding it?

Yes, provided your soil is not stiff clay. Bolting, as premature seeding is called, generally follows any check to growth due to cold or drought. Try a non-bolting variety such as Avonearly or Boltardy. Soak the seed for 48 hours and then sow in a warm part of the garden. The ground should not have been freshly manured or the roots will fork, but it should have had peat raked in to improve moisture-holding and it will need a general fertilizer. Water in dry weather.

106

WHAT is the best treatment for attacks of mildew on swede turnips? Does this make the roots unfit to put into store?

The mildew will be on the leaves, which you remove before putting the roots into store, so storage should not be a problem. The variety Marian resists mildew extremely well. If the attack is severe, the plants can be sprayed with zineb, but normally the mildew comes too late to affect the size of the crop and is not severe enough to be a menace.

107

WHY do my carrots, which are kept clear of pests, by routine spraying, suddenly all split their sides?

Not with laughing! But perhaps because they have suffered severe thirst. When heavy rain follows drought, the core swells rapidly, but the outer flesh, having dried out in the drought, is unable to stretch, so it splits.

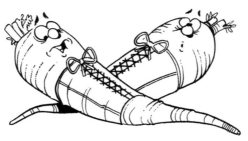

108

WHAT can be done to avoid trouble in carrots which have been sown too thickly? It is difficult to sow the seed thinly enough, and when the seedlings are thinned out the disturbance attracts the carrot fly. Since soil pesticides spoil the taste, what is the solution?

Modern granular insecticides such as bromophos and diazinon do not taint the crop so they can be used safely. When thinning the seedlings, do it just before dark when the fly is not active, and clear away the thinnings promptly. That way the smell, released by handling the plants has time to clear considerably before the flies get busy the next morning.

109

WHY do cauliflower leaves become distorted and narrow instead of normal shape? Why at the same time do the heads fail to develop? There are no pests and the soil is good.

This is a disorder known as Whiptail and is caused by lack of molybdenum. Water with sodium molybdate, at one ounce to two gallons over ten square yards. And lime the ground in winter before planting cauliflowers.

110

WILL it be necessary to break a leaf over the curd to keep winter cauliflowers white, the same as is done to keep the sunshine off summer cauliflower?

Yes, when the curds develop. Winter light is strong enough to turn the curds yellow. Also, in winter the plants should be set to lean well to the north. To do this, remove some soil from the north side, push the plant over, and press some soil against the south side of the stem.

111

WHAT is the difference between broccoli and cauliflower?

Botanically none. In practice, single-headed winter cauliflower used to be called broccoli but now all single-headed, summer or winter, are called cauliflower, and the sprouting type are called broccoli.

112

WHEN pigeons pecked the centres out of my spring cabbages, three or four little cabbages started to form on each stalk. Is it worth while keeping these plants and allowing the new hearts to grow?

Yes, you can eat the baby cabbage as soon as the leaves are big enough to be worth cutting. Or you can leave them to form small hearts in June. Nitrate of soda at an ounce to the yard run will hasten growth if applied in March. But the problem indicates a need to take action before the pigeons get to work: action to keep them off.

113

WHAT is the best remedy for Cabbage Root Fly? My summer cabbage was ruined by the root fly maggot and to protect my autumn crop I was advised to put a tarred disc around each plant. What are these made of?

You can make tarred discs from six-inch rings of felt or cardboard soaked in neat tar-oil wash. There must be a circular hole in the middle of each disc and a slit from middle to edge so that the disc can be slipped into place. I don't know that there is any "best" remedy. Tarred discs keep the fly away and there are several soil insecticides which will kill the maggots – such as bromophos or diazinon.

114

WHAT is the heaviest cabbage ever recorded? What kind was it and what was its weight?

The famous Swalwell Cabbage grown by Bill Collingwood at Swalwell, on Tyneside in 1865 was reputed to weigh 123 lbs and as far as I know has never been equalled. This was a red cabbage, the type which is popular for pickling. There were no record books published at that time but there are such books today, of which those sponsored by Guinness are the best known. The way to keep in touch with achievements is to check the latest editions.

115

HOW can clubroot disease be controlled? The trouble was carried into my garden on some winter cabbages which were a gift.

It is wise to be careful and to be wary of gift cabbages because clubroot fungus, once you find it in the garden, will be with you for years, living in the soil. To help contain it, practice crop rotation; keep the ground clear of plant debris; start all brassica seedlings in sterilized compost; and treat the seedlings with calomel when planting. This will not eradicate the fungus but it helps brassica crops get established before they become infected and thus it gives a chance of reasonable crops.

116

WHAT are the small dirty-white maggots on the roots of Brussels sprouts? Are they the cause of the collapse of the plants? What is the preventive treatment?

The pests are grubs of the Cabbage Root Fly. They have hatched from eggs laid in the soil by the fly. Dust the soil around sprouts and other brassicas with HCH or a proprietary soil insecticide to keep off the fly, or use tarred discs on the ground around the stems. When the maggots are hatching, a soil insecticide such as HCH, or bromophos or diazinon can be helpful.

117

WILL it help Brussels sprout plants make better sprouts if some of the leaves are removed and at what stage?

Not much, but the lowest leaves should be snapped off as they yellow. Firm ground is the key to firm sprouts.

118

WHEN picking Brussels sprouts, does it matter whether one starts at the bottom of the stem or at the top?

It is important that you start at the bottom. It is equally important that you take a few sprouts from the bottom of each plant, and remove the lowest leaves as you go, rather than strip any plant. A brief study of a Brussels sprout plant in the early stage of sprout development is enough to let you see that the lowest sprouts swell up first, though there are some varieties where the difference is not so great.

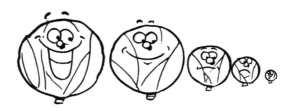

119

HOW can one pick Brussels sprouts when plants are frozen solid? After growing lovely Brussels sprouts, I find that in the worst weather, when they are dear in the shops, I cannot pick any. Apart from the risk of frostbite, the sprouts might go black and soft if handled while frozen?

With a deep freezer one can have them available whenever needed, without having to pick them in frosty weather. But by the time severe frosts arrive, there must be plenty of plants on which every remaining sprout is big enough. In that event, chop down a whole plant, cut off the leaves and (without touching the sprouts) thaw the plant in COLD water in the kitchen sink. Then just break them off at the stem.

120

HOW can I avoid white-fly on brassica crops? My cabbages and sprouts look clean until touched, and then clouds of white insects fly out, similar to greenhouse white-fly.

Cabbage whitefly is a hardier creature than greenhouse whitefly but is just as difficult to shift. The pest works on the undersides of the leaves and is hard to get at. Most growers just accept it, if the infestation is not too bad. But it can be kept within bounds by spraying with resmethrin.

121

WHY do some brassica plants have large colonies of horrible little grey lice on them when others are clear? What are these lice and how does one treat them?

This is the Cabbage Mealy aphid, and should be sprayed with malathion or similar pesticide. Repeat as needed.

122

WHAT can one do to get rid of those little maggots which eat the radishes, without spoiling the radishes? I got rid of some by using a dust called HCH, but this dust gives the radishes an awful taste.

HCH is a new name for BHC (Lindane) dust which should not be used on root crops, because it taints. Non-tainting modern pesticides include bromophos, chlorpyrifos, and diazinon, and these can be used whenever there are signs that the pests are active. All the same, radish is a quick-growing subject, and if encouraged, should be ready before pests have time to do damage.

123

WHY are outdoor cucumbers such unattractive, little, fat, prickly things?

They are not, or at least not all of them. Anyway we can't all be beautiful as well as useful. What you describe are the old hardy RIDGE cucumbers, which are tasty despite their looks. But there are LONG outdoor varieties such as Nadir, Greenline, and Baton Vert available nowadays, and their skins are nearly as smooth as those of the indoor types.

124

HOW can I avoid having so many lettuce wasted through going to seed? Whatever variety I sow, I seem to harvest only a couple before the rest bolt.

Lettuce likes rich soil with enough fibre in it to prevent its drying out. Try sowing in the row, to avoid a transplanting check. Such checks can cause bolting. Also, it is better to sow a tiny pinch of seed each week than to sow enough at a time to last a month. Try the variety Salad Bowl. It is not a hearting variety; you pick it leaf by leaf, and it is slow to bolt.

125

WHEN my lettuce runs to seed prematurely, should I discard it or leave it to make seed? Is there any way of deciding which is the best one to keep for seed?

Judging the best seed in the normal way means choosing and marking the best plant before it seeds. But when a plant goes to seed PREMATURELY it is unwise to save the seed, because it will almost certainly produce plants with the same weakness as the parents — they will be seedy.

126

WILL potatoes grow satisfactorily without ridging up the soil over them, or are they liable to go green?

One method some people use is to spread black polythene, about two feet or so wide, on the ground, Slash x-shaped cuts a foot apart and plant a potato, barely covered with soil, in each cut. You MUST put slug pellets under the polythene. Hold down the sheet with stones and a bit of soil along the edges. To harvest the potatoes you put your hand under the sheet and pick them off as needed. This is the chief advantage of the method. But potatoes in open soil are often grown without earthing up. I don't think the risk of greening is much greaer than with the ridging method, but ridging does help to support the stems.

127

WHAT is the reason why some people spread newspaper over the plants when early potatoes show above the surface? Is it necessary?

The earliest plantings are liable to break surface before spring frost risk is over. Normal practice then is just to draw soil over. Keep repeating this until the soil is well ridged up, and by that time frosts should be over. Where potatoes have been fully ridged before frosts have finished, the paper is put on in the evenings when frost threatens, and must be removed in the mornings to allow the plants enough light.

128

WHEN growing maincrop potatoes, where there is obviously no great hurry, is it essential to get potatoes sprouting before planting?

Not essential, but advisable. It helps eliminate blind and diseased tubers (those which fail to sprout) and also enables the gardener to rub off surplus shoots and so avoid excessive top-growth. Too many stems may mean more potatoes but may also mean too many under-sized ones. Three is the maximum number of shoots that should be left on each tuber when planting. A rough rule is: to get big potatoes, leave only one shoot; for medium to large, two shoots; for medium, three; and for small, four. But varieties differ and one must be familiar with the variety before being too precise.

129

WHEN those green tomato-like fruits appear on potato tops are they seed fruits? And can the seed be sown the following year to produce a crop of potatoes?

They are definitely seed fruits and each seed will produce a plant which in turn will make one small potato tuber. But you could not expect a worthwhile crop that way. To get a crop, you would need to save those little potatoes you grow from the seed, and plant them out the following year.

130

WHY is it considered best to stand seed potatoes "rose" end upwards on trays, to sprout before planting? And what is meant by the "rose" end?

The rose end is the opposite end of the potato from that which was attached to the root. And it is the end on which one expects to find the most and best "eyes" – points from which sprouts (growth shoots) will come.

131

WHY do my potatoes start sprouting prematurely in store? Could I stop it by bringing them into the light in the cool greenhouse?

They sprout because they are not cold enough. If they are for eating, you must keep them in the dark, because light turns them green and uneatable. Just keep them in as cool a store-place as you can find. Full light would slow down the sprout growth, and is correct for tubers which are to be planted as "seed". Greening will not do them any harm for that purpose.

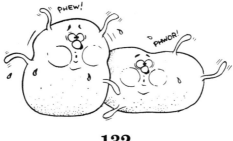

132

WHY am I constantly advised to use only "certified" seed potatoes? Since they are expensive I should like to save some of my own but I do not want to do the wrong thing.

Once-saved seed (first-year tubers grown from certified stock) are not a great risk if the plants on which they grew were healthy. "Certified" tubers are free from virus infection to which potatoes are highly suspectible. These viruses are not detectable in the tuber at planting time and infected tubers are liable to fail. So "certified" tubers are safest; "once-saved" are a small risk; after that it is a gamble.

133

WHAT is the difference between new potatoes and main-crop varieties?

The term "new" is applied to immature tubers, dug before they reach full size. Usually these are early varieties (quick growers) but they CAN be from maincrop. Maincrop varieties are slower to mature than early varieties and, when matured, will keep better than earlies.

134

WHAT precautions need one take against blight when growing potatoes and tomatoes in a sheltered garden? Can fungicide be applied from a watering can?

Shelter does not make a garden safe against blight. Use Bordeaux mixture to keep it out, but use a proper sprayer so that you wet the undersides of the leaves as well as the upper surfaces. Potato and tomato plants want the same treatment, because the same blight attacks both.

135

HOW serious is potato scab? I have very sandy soil and my potatoes are scabby. The variety Maris Piper grows and cooks excellently despite being scabby, but I should like a maincrop immune to scab?

If the potatoes are good, as you say, the trouble must be common scab, which is only skin deep and harmless. No variety is completely immune but King Edward and Pentland Crown show strong resistance to scab.

136

WHY did my potato plants suddenly die and produce only a few undersized tubers? They were not short of water. I was told eelworm might be the cause but there is no eelworm to be seen.

The symptoms fit potato cyst eelworm, but the pest is not noticeable to the naked eye. It infests the soil for years, so you should plant only resistant varieties. Switch the potato plot each year and plant fresh, certified seed always.

137

WHEN potato plants come into flower does this indicate that the potatoes are ready for digging?

Yes, but you don't always have to wait, because some varieties are shy at flowering and the tubers are ready before the plants flower. If an early variety has been planted 12 weeks, it is worth digging one root to examine the tubers.

138

WHAT causes potatoes to have a small patch of rot in the middle that is not evident until the potato is cut open?

It is normally due to the weather – to an erratic water supply. Drought followed by heavy rain creates a hole in the middle (called Hollow Heart) which tends to rot.

139

HOW harmful is lime to potatoes? I was advised to use a 50-50 mixture of lime and copper sulphate at one ounce to the sq. yard, against slugs on my potato patch. But I am told that lime would make the potatoes scabby.

Lime in substantial quantities might irritate the skin of the potatoes and cause scab, but the lime in the treatment described is only about one thirtieth of a routine lime application, and will do no harm.

140

WHEN working to a crop rotation, can potatoes follow cabbages, if the patch was limed for the cabbages?

Yes. Although potatoes do not like an alkaline soil they can go into ground limed the previous year.

141

WHY do potatoes (variety Majestic) look excellent when peeled but turn blackish when cooked? Does it indicate something wrong with the cultivation?

Majestic does sometimes tend to darken when cooked where other varieties might not. But the trouble can appear in any variety, where there is too much iron in the soil or in the cooking water. A squeeze of lemon in the cooking water should keep the potatoes white.

142

WHAT causes potatoes (such as Ulster Chieftain and Pentland Javelin) to disintegrate when cooking? Is it because the soil lacks something?

No. Good cooking can help you avoid this trouble, which is often due to fast boiling. Put the potatoes into a pan of COLD, salted water; bring it to the boil; then turn down the heat so as just to simmer.

143

WHY is it that despite regular and heavy applications of fertilizer to my runner beans, the plants give only a small crop of beans?

There may be several factors such as lack of humus in the soil, lack of moisture, and cold weather. But the trouble could be due to excessive use of fertilizers. This would produce big leaves at the expense of beans. Give just one application, at sowing time, at the rate prescribed on the bag.

144

WHAT causes runner beans to go droopy, and to climb just a little way up the pole and then hang down? Also the flowers seem to fall and not make pods.

It suggests lack of moisture in the soil and in the air. If the plants are otherwise healthy, they are probably in need of a soaking. Thirsty plants lack the vigour to climb. A dry atmosphere causes flowers to drop, so syringe the plants on dry days.

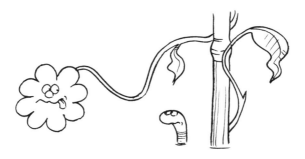

145

WHY do my runner bean flowers set hardly any beans despite having bees busy in them all day? Surely that ought to mean good pollination and plenty of beans. I find holes in the flowers which indicates damage by some insect.

The way bees pollinate the blooms is accidental. They push out their tongues to reach past the pollen to the nectar and in so doing transfer the pollen. Short-tongued bees can't reach the nectar in that way so they bite a hole near the base of the flower and get straight to the nectar. What happens next is that the long-tongued bees then use the same hole, so that there is none of the normal accidental movement of pollen – and no beans.

146

WHEN the catalogue tells me that my runner beans will grow to 18 inches long and I am urged to pick them small (say a foot long), what should I do?

The catalogue is describing size at maturity but you should pick them small if you want to be sure of fleshy, tender pods. Bean size is variable, but it is best to pick them less than a foot long, or before the pods bulge to show the swelling of the seeds.

147

WILL broadbeans escape attack by blackfly if sown early – say February?

There is no guarantee, but February sowings ought to mature before the blackfly (Bean aphid) becomes active. At worst, aphid damage will be insignificant if the tips of the plants are nipped out at the first sign of attack. The young tip growth is the main attraction for the pest.

148

WHAT is the correct thing to do with pea plants after the pea pods have been harvested? Some people say pull out the plants and burn them but others say compost them or dig them in.

The tops should be chopped off and either put on the compost heap or dug in to make humus. The roots contain nodules of nitrogen and should be left in the ground to enrich the soil.

149

WILL it harm peas if they are soaked in paraffin before sowing? Newly-sown peas are regularly dug out and eaten by mice and I understand that paraffin would keep them off.

Do NOT soak the peas in paraffin or they will be ruined. The drill is to shake them in a spoonful of paraffin in a jar for a few seconds before sowing, but that is all. This will keep the mice off, but you could try to get rid of the mice by trapping or by using a rat bait.

150

WHY do peas suddenly wither and die, despite being properly watered, in a spot where they have done well previously?

This is, most likely, fusarium wilt. Peas must not be sown in the same spot year after year, nor in one used the previous year for beans. Fusarium lives in the soil but can be avoided by proper crop rotation.

151

WHEN sowing peas in June, it would seem logical to sow a late variety, since the aim is a late crop. However I understand early varieties are recommended for this late sowing. Why is this?

"Early" does not indicate season of year but quickness of maturing. And the later the season of sowing the quicker we may need to be. That is why earlies are the rule for June sowings.

152

WHEN is the best time to plant onion sets? I realise that the sooner they go in the bigger they can grow, since they have their fixed time of ripening but I don't want to start too early.

You are right in all respects. It is wise to avoid early plantings because they are liable to be checked by a cold spell, and run to seed; even though ideally the longer they have, the bigger they can grow. Mid-March is early enough and it should never be attempted if the weather or soil is not right.

153

WHY do my two varieties of onion sets – both from reputable firms – go to seed even after being kept back till late March before planting?

Ideally, sets must be kept cool and preferably in full light while waiting to be planted. This can be a problem when temperatures fluctuate, but keeping them cold really is the priority. It seems probable that fluctuating or over-high temperature before planting, or a cold snap after planting, must have affected them.

154

WHAT causes onions, grown from sets, to split at the base when they appear otherwise healthy?

This trouble is called Saddleback and is due to unsuitable weather. A spell of dry weather toughens the bulb, and then when heavy rain follows, the bulb splits, instead of stretching. The remedy is never to let onions go dry, especially in June or July.

155

WHAT is the rule about pollinating cucumbers and marrows?

These two plants are treated quite differently. Marrows may need pollinating — by transferring pollen from the male flower to the female (the female flowers have tiny marrows behind them). But cucumbers should NOT be pollinated, or the fruits will be ugly and bitter. So all male cucumber flowers should be removed promptly. Again it is easy to tell the difference between male and female, because there is a tiny cucumber behind the female flower.

156

HOW does one feed the fruit directly (not through the roots) to fatten a vegetable marrow for a giant-marrow competition?

Put a teaspoonful of sugar in a pint of water in a bottle. Thread wool through the neck of the marrow and lead it into the bottle. Keep the bottle neck close to the marrow. Refill as needed. The wool acts like blotting paper to drain up the liquid from the bottle and the marrow fruit is able to digest it. But if there is too much space between the bottle neck and the marrow, the wool will dry out instead of channelling the liquid.

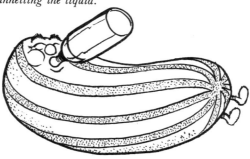

157

WHY is it necessary to pinch out the growing tips of trailing-type vegetable marrows? and when should it be done?

Because the marrow fruits are produced on side-shoots, so the growth of these should be encouraged and speeded by pinching out the tip of the main stem. Pinching also makes a much more compact plant. Do it when the stem is two feet long. Later pinch out the tips of side shoots when they get too long after fruits have formed.

158

WHAT causes fruits of cucumbers to wither at the blossom end when about two inches long, and then fall off?

This failure usually indicates that the soil is too wet, and probably too cold. The plant should get over the trouble if watering is corrected.

159

WHY should some cucumber fruits taste bitter even after all the male flowers have been carefully removed to prevent pollination?

Pollination is not the only cause of bitter fruits. The fault can follow sudden changes in temperature or humidity. If such a fruit is cut two or three inches from the tip, and the cut surfaces are rubbed together, the bitter taste usually disappears. Fruits which are pollinated usually swell near the ends and the bitterness in these fruits is not easy to eradicate.

160

WHY does summer spinach go to seed? Mine seems to do it regardless of the weather.

Spinach likes to grow rapidly. It resents hot conditions, or light, sandy soil which dries too quickly. Add extra humus to the soil; choose a site which gets a little shade if possible in the heat of the day, but always give water during a dry spell.

161

WHAT is the right direction for vegetable rows to run? and does it really matter?

It is not a critical matter, but if the rows run north-south the sun can get to both sides of the row in the course of the day. If the rows run east to west, rows of taller plants will put adjoining rows in the shade, and how much that matters depends on the depth of the shade. Most people try to keep the rows running north to south.

162

HOW much salt should I apply each year to an asparagus bed? I have heard that salt at one part in a thousand can be bad for plants.

One part salt in a thousand parts soil can be harmful, though not seriously in such small measure. The practice of putting salt on asparagus is out of date. It does no good for the plants and it can damage the soil structure. Hence it is no longer recommended or practised by the best authorities.

163

WHAT makes mint shrivel and go rusty-orange colour, despite repeated changes of site to various parts of the garden? Even burning it off does not seem to clean up the plants of this trouble.

This is a fungus trouble called Mint Rust and infected plants should be dug up and put on the incinerator. You need fresh clean plants and it is wise to change the mint bed every three years to reduce risk of severe infection.

164

HOW thick a layer of compost do I need to spread on my vegetable plot? I understand that if I spread compost on the surface each year I can cut out the hard work of digging, and I should like to try it.

Compost gardening as an alternative to digging is NOT a work-saver. You need a two-inch mulch of compost, which means about 16 cub. yds., for a standard allotment of 300 sq. yards. Spreading that, is more work than digging. It certainly brings good results for those who have the muscle.

Chapter Three

Fruit

165

WHAT causes patches of waxy "cotton wool" on apple trees? and will it do any harm after the fruit has been picked?

This "cotton wool" contains a bug called woolly aphid. Canker, which is a serious disease, enters wounds on shoots damaged by this pest. You can brush out each patch of wool with a small brush dipped in methylated spirit. Insecticides can be used but must be sprayed with some force to make them penetrate the "wool" and reach the bug.

166

HOW can one keep birds (tits in particular) from damaging fruit on apple trees? Deterrents don't seem to work.

The tits feed on insects, so spraying to keep aphids and caterpillars under control will greatly reduce bird damage. Penitrothion is a useful insecticide against both aphids and caterpillars.
N.B. This spraying can be used to protect other types of fruit trees.

167

WHEN the cut ends of branches on apple trees go reddish brown all round the edges of the cut, does it indicate disease?

It suggests canker. Infected branches must be cut back to clean wood which does not turn brown. The cut end should be treated with canker paint.

168

WHY do two apple trees, a Cox and a Bramley, blossom profusely every year but hardly ever produce a reasonable quality of fruit from the Cox?

They probably need a pollinator. Bramley cannot pollinate anything because genetically it is triploid, whereas pollinators should be diploid. So your Cox has not much chance unless bees bring in suitable pollen from neighbouring gardens. It would help if another variety, such as Worcester were planted near.

169

WHICH sort of spray is best to get rid of a white powder – presumably mildew – on the leaves of apple trees?

Firstly, where the mildew is mainly on the tips of shoots, the tips can be cut off and destroyed. Where this is not enough, spray with dinocap or similar fungicide, and repeat as needed.

170

WHY do small, brown, corky spots form under the skin of apples which externally are quite unblemished?

This is a physiological disorder called Bitter Pit, and is usually due to shortage of calcium. But it can be caused also by unbalanced feeding or erratic water supply.

171

HOW is it that an apple tree (Egremont Russet) can have its blooms killed by frost when other varieties in the next door garden survive and make fruit?

Frost does sometimes strike in strange ways due to air currents. But Egremont blooms early and may catch frost which later bloomers escape, and this is the most likely explanation. Late-blooming, healthy, varieties include Discovery, Epicure, Worcester Pearmain, and Red Ellison.

172

WILL apples store safely in a slightly damp store-room built on the back of a garage?

Yes, unless it is too damp and mouldy. Apples don't like an over-dry atmosphere. Chiefly they must be stored cool (about 38°F), so there is scope for ventilation, which could clear excessive dampness.

173

WHY do swarms of ants attack apple trees when they are a mass of bloom, causing damage to both blossom and leaves?

Ants would not eat blossoms or leaves. They would probably be after aphids. Caterpillars are probably to blame for some of the damage. Spraying with derris or fenitrothion, at bud burst and again just before the blossoms open should take care of both these pests and the ants will then go elsewhere.

174

WHAT insecticide is safest to use when wasps are eating apples which are approaching ripeness?

Spraying the trees would not help much at such a stage. It is better to watch at dusk and see where the wasps go to nest. Some types nest in the ground and some in trees or buildings. There are proprietary brands of wasp killer which can be put into the nest just before dark, when the wasps are all in. HCH or Derris are suitable wasp killers.

175

HOW does one get rid of the maggot which is found in the core of an apple? I don't begrudge the maggot his bite but there's nothing worse than biting an apple and seeing a maggot in it.

There is. Seeing half a maggot after you take a bite is worse! It is too late to start any attack on the pest once it is in there. The maggot is probably the caterpillar of the Codling Moth and it is the moth, not the caterpillar, which we must attack. Spray the tree with malathion four weeks after blossom fall and repeat the spray three weeks later.

176

WHEN a so-called "dwarf" apple tree goes on growing year after year, and not producing any blossom, should it be cut hard?

No. The likely explanation is that the tree has been planted too deeply, burying the graft, so that it is now growing on its own roots and losing the dwarfing influence of the rootstock. The danger is that the rootstock will have died. You can dig it up and see. If the dwarfing root is still viable, trim off the scion roots and replant at the correct depth.

177

WHAT is meant by a "three-cultivar" pear tree?

Cultivar is a botanical term for a variety produced by man rather than in nature. Three-cultivar means three varieties on one tree. Fruit trees like this are produced by making three separate grafts. The main branch which has grown out from each graft should be labelled so that you know which variety is growing on which part of the tree.

178

WHY do pears, such as Williams and Conference, always seem mealy when picked?

They don't, if picked at the proper time. Mealiness indicates that they have been left to ripen on the tree. Williams should be picked green and hard, usually late August, and Conference late September. All pears should be picked at their own proper stage of ripeness and should complete their ripening after picking.

179

HOW can one avoid having wholesome pears pecked by birds? After waiting till the right time for picking, it is annoying to find every one ruined by pecks.

Picking cannot be altered to save the pecks. The best answer is to make a round cardboard disc for each pear. Cut a slit in each disc from outside edge to centre, so that it can be slipped over the stalk like an umbrella. This keeps birds off and allows the fruit to complete its development.

180

WHAT makes leaves of a plum tree shine like aluminium? When it happens to only one branch, should this branch be cut off and burned? And is it safe to cut a thick branch when the tree is in fruit?

The trouble is Silver Leaf Fungus, and June/July with the tree in fruit is the right time to cut, because the fungus is least active then. The infected branch should be cut back to clean, white wood and the cut should be treated immediately with a canker paint.

181

WHEN the bark of a plum tree splits from top to bottom on one side of the trunk, can it be revived?

The tree needs no reviving. The bark splits because it has got too dry, probably during or after transplanting. Treat the split with tree paint or lead paint.

182

HOW should one treat a greengage tree that is sending up shoots at a distance of up to 12 feet from the trunk? Are these shoots harmful to the tree?

The shoots are suckers which will rob the tree of nourishment and could even starve it to death. They should be cut clean out from the main root.

183

WHAT is the black substance which forms on the leaves of a plum tree and also falls on the grass beneath?

It is a fungus called Sooty Mould, which grows on the honeydew from aphids. The remedy is to tackle the aphids, not the Sooty Mould. Spray with systemic insecticide and repeat if needed. Before blossom time each season, and at blossom fall, give this spray as a regular routine till the trouble is eliminated.

184

WHEN a branch of a plum tree breaks under the weight of fruit, what can be done, bearing in mind that plums must not be pruned at certain times because of the risk of Silver Leaf fungus?

Although plums are normally pruned only in July to reduce risk of Silver Leaf, one can't ignore a broken branch, which may be infected anyway. It must be removed promptly as soon as it is found to have broken, and the wound treated thoroughly with canker paint.

185

WHAT is the cure for a Victoria plum tree which has healthy leaves and carries a wonderful crop but has blobs of glue on most of the branches?

When it occurs in an otherwise healthy tree, this gumming suggests under-nourishment. Feeding with a high-potash fertilizer in January should help to correct it. Paint the blobs with tar oil (fruit tree winter wash) to ward off fungus attacks.

186

WHEN is the best time to cut back a walnut tree which is 30 feet tall with a 25-ft spread? Branches are overhanging a neighbour's garden.

Walnut trees should not be cut when dormant but only when in full leaf, probably in May. Cuts should be dusted with powdered charcoal till dry, then painted with Arbex tree paint. If the tree is cut in winter it is liable to bleed to death. In any event, do not be too severe, but cut back only as much as is essential.

187

HOW far can one take seriously the old English proverb: "A woman, a dog and a walnut tree, the more you beat them the better they'll be"? Will beating make the tree more fruitful?

No. Beating the tree is done to get off unripe nuts for pickling. The beating serves no other useful purpose. As for the woman and the dog, well that is just a laugh.

188

WHAT is the best way to grow peach trees from seed? Does one crack the stone?

Put a handful of peach stones in a pot of sand and plunge the pot to its brim in the soil for winter frost to split the stones. In March, each seed that is sprouting is put into a small pot. Non-sprouters can then be cracked to help them out, if they are wanted.

189

WHY do the leaves of peach trees turn reddish and crinkled just after the blossom withers? Why do insecticides fail at that stage and when is the right time to spray?

The disease is Peach Leaf Curl and insecticides won't help because it is a fungus. Spray with Bordeaux mixture or Nimrod-T fungicide twice in February. A further spray is needed in the autumn, when the leaves begin to fall.

190

WILL fruit grow on an orange tree raised from a pip and grown in a ten-inch pot?

It is difficult to predict how long a summer will be needed for an orange grown from seed to make fruit. Much depends on its ancestors. But the tree wants all the sunlight possible. Home conditions are not light enough, so the tree is best put outdoors in summer in a sheltered, sunny position.

191

WHAT chance is there of getting chestnuts from a chestnut tree which has been grown from a conker?

What we call "conkers" are seeds of the horse chestnut and the tree should certainly produce these when it is mature. But the chestnuts for roasting and eating are of an entirely different family. They are the Sweet or Spanish Chestnut (Castanea). That is where castanets get their name – being made from the wood of sweet chestnuts. The horse chestnut is an Aesculus.

192

WHEN growing strawberries under cloches how soon should the cloches be put over the plants to get an early crop?

Normal time is about mid-February, but it depends on the weather. The aim is to put the cloches on at the end of a cold spell, so that the plants get a double dose of extra warmth to hurry them on.

193

HOW frequently do we need to remove cloches over strawberries to give the soil a thorough watering?

Not at all. Soil under cloches looks dry when it is moist underneath. Rain falling alongside soaks up to the plant roots. The same applies with artificial watering. So in extremely dry weather you can spray water on the cloches and not bother to move them.

194

WHY is it necessary to put straw around strawberry plants?

It isn't, but without it you might get your teeth full of grit, from soil splashes, when eating the fruit. A square of polythene, slit from one edge to the middle can be slipped under each plant instead. And under cloches no ground cover is needed because the cloches prevent splashing. When straw or polythene is put on the ground precautions must be taken against slugs, which would hide under it.

195

WHICH chemical can be used to control the mould called botrytis on strawberries without tainting the fruit and without interfering with harvesting?

Most chemicals have restrictions on use near picking time and it is important to watch them carefully. There are several that can be used up to a week before picking. Plants treated with benomyl, which is effective against botrytis, are not tainted and the fruit can be picked the same day as it is sprayed.

196

WHEN strawberries are covered by cloches to keep birds off and are kept clear of slugs, what pest makes peck marks on some of the fruits?

Most likely it is the Strawberry Beetle, which is not normally a serious menace. But when fruiting is finished, it is wise to remove the cloches, clear out ALL weeds, and let the birds catch any beetles that are there.

197

WHAT special treatment is needed by strawberries planted in five-inch pots of rich compost in a cold greenhouse to get early crops?

The most important point is to put them OUTSIDE until about early February and let them suffer some hard weather. Otherwise they will not fruit well. When they are brought indoors, spray them then with fenitrothion and give them a high-potash plant food.

198

WILL it weaken or damage the plants if all leaves are cut off strawberry plants when fruiting is finished?

No, you can take a rotary mower over the plants if you like. By removing and burning all old leaves and all unwanted runners you reduce the risk of pests and diseases in the plants.

199

WHY is the tomato classed as a vegetable for show purposes when clearly it is a fruit?

The Royal Horticultural Society rule is that for show purposes a plant normally grown in the kitchen garden is a vegetable unless it is eaten as a sweet. An interesting exception is rhubarb. Though it is commonly eaten as a sweet, it is classed as a vegetable in shows.

200

WHAT truth is there in the tale that sometimes you can hear rhubarb growing?

You can't hear it in the garden. But in the darkened forcing sheds, where rhubarb is grown commercially the leaves rub and swish each other as they open, and they make quite an eerie noise.

201

WHAT is the rule about cutting rhubarb?
First of all, it should never be cut. The stalks should be pulled cleanly

away at the base. Never leave the plant with fewer than four good stems, to keep it growing. If flower stems develop they should be removed promptly.

202

HOW important is aspect when planting a grape vine outside a greenhouse and leading the fruiting stems inside? If the only planting space is on the dark, north side of the greenhouse will this do?

The position of roots is not critical. Good soil and good drainage are more important than aspect. Anyway, a vine trained in through the north end of a greenhouse will be growing towards the sun and should be quite happy.

203

WHAT causes a young grape vine in a greenhouse, with masses of bunches, to fail to swell its grapes and just to let them crumble away?

This trouble is called "shanking" and can be caused by poor or dry soil or over-cropping. A young vine allowed to carry a large number of bunches will be over-loaded and that could cause the shanking.

204

WHY must raspberry canes, planted in November, be cut down immediately to six inches, bearing in mind it would mean no fruit the following season?

They are cut down to six inches to help new growth. Although this means sacrificing fruit for the first year, it is a very small sacrifice because the young plants would have only one two-foot cane each. And the important thing is to let the plants concentrate on making some good canes to carry the second full season's crop.

205

WHAT is wrong with raspberries when, after cropping well, many of the canes at the end of the season look tired, with leaves losing colour, while some look bright and green?

Probably nothing. The bright ones most likely are new canes which will fruit the following year. The weary ones will be those which have just cropped and have had their day. Cut these down to ground level after the fruit is picked.

206

HOW does one take cuttings of a thornless blackberry, planted four years ago, which has made magnificent growth and is a wonderful cropper? and when is the best time to do it?

August is the best time but don't take cuttings. Propagation is best done by what is called tip layering. Just push the ends of shoots into the ground about six inches and peg them down. Make a slit in the ground with the spade to let the tip in easily. The tips will root and make new stems. You can sever the plantlets from the mother shoots, in the following spring.

207

WHAT can be done about mildew on gooseberries when it is near picking time and normal fungicides would make the fruits risky to eat? Is there a safe treatment or must one wait till the berries are harvested?

A harmless fungicide you can use is washing soda at one pound to five gallons of water. Better try that rather than leave the fungus untreated, since berries attacked by the fungus could soon become uneatable.

208

WHEN two-year-old gooseberry bushes make new stems from ground level should one encourage them, to make the plants more bushy, or is there reason to remove them?

Gooseberry bushes are normally trained on a single "leg" or mainstem. Those extra shoots would crowd the bush and the berries would probably be mouldy through lack of air circulation. If they are springing from the soil, sever them clean off at the roots. Any part of the shoot left on would grow out again.

209

HOW severely should blackcurrants be pruned and when is the best time to do it?

Older wood on blackcurrant bushes does not fruit well, so as much of it as possible should be cut out immediately the crop is picked. Cut every stem down to a lowly-placed new side-shoot. Also remove any weak or badly-placed shoot. A simple system is to cut the fruiting stems clean off before removing the fruit. That way, pruning and picking are done in one operation and the picker can sit down to handle the loaded stems instead of stooping over the bush.

210

WHAT causes blackcurrant bushes to have hollow stems? When stems are pruned, some are found to have holes bored down the centre, presumably by a pest.

Those tunnels in the stems are made by the caterpillar of the Currant Shoot Borer which is inaccessible to chemical sprays while it is at work. Infested parts of stems should be removed and destroyed by burning.

211

WHEN Big Bud attacks blackcurrants can it be cured by removing the buds?

'Big Bud' indicates the presence of a microscopic pest called gall mite. If infested buds are removed and put on the fire promptly, the pest can be kept under control but watch must be kept every year, as this treatment will not eliminate the pest.

212

WHAT is the difference between Burgundy mixture and Bordeaux mixture? I should like the formula to make Burgundy Mixture for spraying a grape vine while it is dormant.

To make Burgundy Mixture, dissolve (in water) in separate buckets, four ounces of copper sulphate and five ounces of washing soda. Mix the two solutions together and add more water to make up five gallons. Bordeaux mixture is a similar formula except that it contains lime instead of soda.

Chapter Four

Pot Plants

213

WHAT can I do to make cut flowers last a long time in water? Will sugar in the water do any good?

Cut flowers have a cut-short life. There is a substance called Chrysal which can be put in the water. This gives cut flowers the same length of life as they would have if left growing on the plant. I don't really think sugar does any good though some people swear by it. All sorts of things have their followers, including aspirin, but Chrysal is the only one I have proved effective.

214

HOW should I treat an exotic pot plant called aechmea, after flowering? It has a side shoot and I have been told to pot this up and throw away the old plant but this does not sound right.

It is quite common practice. Cut off the side shoot with a sharp knife and dust it with sulphur before potting. You CAN keep the old plant as well if you wish. It may not bloom again but it will produce more side shoots for you to propagate.

215

WHAT can I do to save a recently-acquired pot plant called Weeping Fig? Despite a warm, bright spot and careful watering, several leaves have yellowed and died already.

There is no need to shed tears over your Weeping Fig. It sulks every time it is moved — even just across the room — and when it sulks, it drops its leaves. It will recover if left alone for a while.

216

HOW true is it that the pot-plant called Aspidistra will survive unlimited neglect and ill-treatment?

Aspidistra is known as the cast-iron plant because it will stand neglect. Nevertheless it responds to GOOD treatment such as regular watering, feeding during the growing season, having the dust taken off its leaves, and so on. This sort of care will give it bright, shiny leaves. Its preference is for a reasonable amount of moisture and the best watering routine is to plunge the pot in a bucket of water and leave it till a minute or so after air bubbles stop coming up. The surplus water should be allowed to drain off before the plant is put back into position. The pot should go near dry before the next watering.

217

WHAT is the method used to produce a pot plant from a pineapple?

Slice the top off the pineapple and press this tufted top into damp sand in a five-inch pot. Keep the sand barely damp. Rooting is slow, so a great deal of patience is needed and the sand must not be allowed to dry out; nor must it be too wet. When the plant has rooted, it can be potted into any proprietary compost.

218

WHAT is the best way to treat a Zebra Plant (Aphelandra) after flowering? Does it need any pruning or re-potting?

When the flower dies, cut back each stem to not more than two pairs of leaves. The right time for repotting is March. This is not an easy plant; but keep it barely moist, and warm, all winter and it will retain its beauty.

219

WHAT causes the leaves of my Winter Cherry to turn yellow and after a while, drop off?

Over-wet soil, dry air, or draughts could be to blame. Give the plant a cosy, well-lit position, and keep the soil just moist. The flowers too are liable to drop without setting their fruits, and the answer to this is to syringe the plants daily with plain water when in flower.

220

WHEN is the best time of year to repot ferns which have overgrown their pots?

The word 'fern' covers more than 10,000 species, but generally potted ferns can be split up in April and the portions can be re-potted separately.

221

WHAT benefit is it to house-plants standing in a window, to be turned daily in order to correct the tendency to one-sided growth?

None really. An occasional turn may be justified to please us rather than to please the plant. But daily turning distorts the plant and does it no good.

222

WHAT is the correct way to treat a pot plant called the Humble Plant, whose leaves fold up when touched?

This plant is Mimosa pudica, and although it is a perennial, it is best treated as an annual. That means it should be grown afresh from seed each year. If you want to keep it for a second year, give it warm, light conditions and water sparingly during winter.

223

HOW should I propagate a houseplant called Chlorophytum, which has slender, striped leaves. It produces baby plants on the ends of long stems and presumably these can be cut off and potted separately. If so, when?

Don't cut them off immediately. Peg each plantlet into a small pot of potting compost strategically placed near to the parent plant. Leave it to get well rooted before you cut the mother stem.

224

WHAT is the correct name of the plant some people call Fat-headed Lizzie? I understood that it is a foliage plant, but have also been told that it may bloom. Is this likely?

The plant is Fatshedera Lizei and it is treated as a foliage plant because its foliage is its attractive feature. Although it sometimes produces pale green flowers in late autumn, these flowers are not significant.

225

WHY is the Money Plant so called and what is its proper name?

Scindapsus aurea is the Money Plant. There is also a succulent, Crassula argentea, known as the Money Tree. Both are supposed to bring luck in the matter of money, but it is all superstition.

226

WHY is Pilea sometimes known as the Aluminium Plant and sometimes as the Friendship Plant?

We are dealing here with two different plants. The plant whose leaves look as if they have been touched up with aluminium is Pilea cadierei. There is another plant called Pilea involucrata, which has pebbly, non-shiny leaves. This is the one known as the Friendship Plant.

It is important to remember that pet names are NOT universally applicable, and the same pet name is given to different plants in different regions.

227

WHAT is the best treatment for the Good Luck Plant? and what is its botanical name?

A succulent called Bryophyllum Daigremontianum, is sometimes called the Good Luck plant. This same plant is often labelled Kalanchoe daigremontianum, and either label is correct. Keep the plant nearly dry in winter, but otherwise it needs no fussing.

228

WHAT is the true Crown of Thorns? The name seems to be given to the houseplant, Euphorbia millii and also to an outdoor shrub called Paliurus.

The houseplant Euphorbia millii is certainly known as Crown of Thorns. But the plant of the Crucifixion, according to Bible scholars, was Paliurus spina-christi – a shrub growing wild in the Holy Land. This is just one of many examples of a popular name used for more than one subject.

229

WHAT is the Curry Plant which is grown in pots and has feathery grey leaves? How can I propagate it?

Helichrysum angustifolium, whose leaves have a curry smell, especially when rubbed is often called the Curry Plant. Cut it down to three or four inches in late spring and root the cuttings. Young plants look best and older plants should be discarded after two seasons.

230

HOW difficult is it to raise geraniums from seed without a garden or a greenhouse?

Not too difficult if you can provide the heat, but it calls for extra patience. You can sow in pots in a warm kitchen or living room in May. The young plants will have to be nursed through the following winter before they will be ready to flower. In a greenhouse, or with the aid of a propagator, an earlier start can be made so that plants reach flowering size in their first year.

231

WHAT is the best way to handle pelargonium cuttings rooted in August and potted singly in three-inch pots, if one is to keep them through the winter, without a greenhouse?

First they should have been pinched back so that they do not go leggy. Avoid icy window-sills or an extremely cold spare room. Give the minimum of water and maximum light. That way they will get through the winter reasonably under normal home conditions.

232

WHAT causes the saucers under my pot plants to have little maggots in them, coming from the soil, and why are there tiny flies on the soil surface at times?

This trouble sounds like the Sciarid Fly (also known as Fungus Gnat) which thrives usually in wet compost containing unsterilized leaf-mould. Water the plants with more care and avoid overwatering. Soak the soil with malathion to kill the pests.

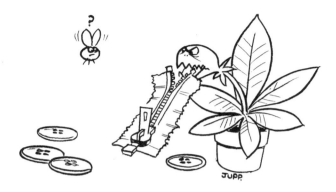

233

WHAT is the name of the pot plant which eats flies?

A plant called Venus's Fly-Trap (Dionaea muscipula) has leaves which hold and consume flies which get on them. But it is not a big eater, so won't keep the house clear of flies. This plant needs a very moist and warm atmosphere and is often disappointing in room conditions.

234

WHAT causes a fine, delicate web on a Castor Oil Plant growing in a sitting room? Could it be the red spiders which are so tiny that I cannot see their legs?

The mites of these tiny red spiders are a menace to plant life. The tiny spiders spin the webs. Spray the plants with resmethrin or other Red Spider Mite spray.

235

WHY is it that despite trying every known remedy for whitefly on house plants, the plants are still smothered in whitefly? Does it mean that the pests developed immunity to the killer spray.

Immunity is unlikely, but whitefly is extremely difficult. Sprays will control the pest, but are not likely to eradicate it unless you spray thoroughly every three days for three weeks (seven sprays). For this you could use resmethrin.

236

WHICH is the better way to water house-plants, just pouring the water on the surface or pouring it into the saucer under the pot?

It makes little difference provided that water is not slopped on carelessly. Whichever way you water, wet the soil thoroughly. And don't leave water in the saucer longer than about half an hour after the watering. Seedlings and baby plants with small root systems, can suffer root disturbance when watered from above, but established plants can stand surface watering.

237

WHEN is the right time of year to transfer house plants from small pots to larger ones to provide extra root room?

It varies according to the subject but generally March or early April is a safe period. If you tap the pot on the bench smartly the plant should lift out cleanly. Then you can examine the root and soil. If the soil is full of roots, re-pot. If not, put it back.

238

WHAT causes some of the outer petals on late flowering chrysan-themums in the greenhouse to go brown? This completely spoils the blooms. Is there any remedy?

The trouble is called petal blight and it happens usually when the air is too damp, due to heavy condensation in autumn temperatures. Spray at the bud stage with Zineb, and give maximum ventilation whenever possible. Once blooms have become blighted, those blooms cannot be saved, but later blooms can be kept clean if the measures described are adopted.

239

WHAT is the cure for collar rot?

There is no cure, apart from trying a fresh laundry! This rot at the base of the stem of a pot plant, must be prevented, or checked in its early stages by treatment with captan or copper dust. The most important precaution against it is to use sterilized compost and to water carefully at all times.

240

WHAT are the ingredients of the special bulb fibre used for the cultivation of bulbs in bowls?

Mix six parts (by volume) of moist peat, with two of oyster-shell grit and one of crushed charcoal. It is important to have the peat reasonably moist before mixing, otherwise it will float to the top when water is added. The oyster shell can be bought from poultry-food stores or pet shops. Charcoal is sold by coal merchants and some plant shops. Thin sticks of wood left in the oven soon become charcoal if a reasonable amount of cooking is done in the oven.

241

HOW frequently should one water bowls of hyacinths which have been started in a cold dark cupboard in a spare room to bloom at Christmas? And how much water should be given each time.

Watering cannot be done by rule of thumb. It demands judgment. Keep the fibre barely moist during the early weeks before the flowers appear. After that they will use a little more water but still must never be wet.

242

WHY do experts advise that newly-planted bowls of bulbs (to flower indoors) should be buried in ashes in a garden frame? Will not this spoil the bowls?

It depends what the bowl is made of, and with pretty bowls it is wiser just to put them in a cool, dark place, such as under the bed in a spare room, provided that it is well ventilated. The aim, as with burying them under ashes, is to keep them cool (but frost-free), and dark, and to reduce risk of rapid drying out. Bowls started under the bed should be checked regularly and lightly watered when necessary but should never be too wet.

243

WHEN hyacinths are forced indoors (in bowls of fibre) to bloom at Christmas, does this exhaust them and make them permanently blind, and of no further use?

They become exhausted because the fibre does not feed them, but if planted in the garden after flowering, they recover and will bloom again after missing one year.

244

WHAT is the best way to treat tiny bulblets produced by sowing seed of hippeastrum? When should they be dried off for their winter rest? How soon will they flower?

The baby bulbs should NOT be dried off, but should be kept growing all the year round until they reach flowering size, which will take about five years. Only after they start flowering do they want an annual short rest.

245

WHEN hippeastrum bulbs are newly planted in pots, should they be put in the dark till they begin sprouting?

No, give them warmth and light. Watering calls for care and skill at this stage, because if the compost is too wet, the base of the bulb will rot instead of rooting. Keep the compost barely moist till two or three inches of growth is made.

246

WHAT causes hippeastrums to fail to flower one year after blooming well the previous year? Should such bulbs be discarded?

*The failure indicates that the bulb was not kept growing strongly for the
few months immediately after flowering. Probably the compost was allowed to
dry out too soon after the flowers faded, which was the time for it to be
manufacturing the next year's blooms. Bulbs which fail should not be discarded.
If kept growing in good, warm conditions they will revive and be ready to flower
again.*

247

WHY do some large-flowered begonias in pots indoors drop their
flowers before they fully open?

*Exceedingly wet compost or very dry air are likely causes. Water carefully,
and stand the pot on pebbles in a bowl with some water in the bottom. Keep the
plants out of draughts and out of direct sun.*

248

WHAT is the proper way to treat a pot plant called achimenes
during the winter? And why is it called Hot Water Plant?

*The small bulb-like tubercles should be allowed to go dry. The pet name is
a clue to the fact that the best way to start the tubercles going again, in early
spring, is to dip them in hot water.*

249

WHEN is the best time to propagate cyclamen? I have one whose
corm is large and I should like to divide it.

*You cannot increase your stock of cyclamen by corm division. The way to
propagate cyclamen is from seed. It is easier if you get ready chitted seed, as you
can do, in spring.*

250

WHY has my cyclamen gone droopy despite being kept moist? I was told to stand it in a bowl of water and pebbles, and I have done so.

From what you say, you must have the pot too wet. Standing permanently in water would make me droopy too. The pot should stand on the pebbles, but the water in the bottom of the bowl should not be deep enough for the pot to touch it. The idea of the water is to maintain a moist atmosphere, and not to water the roots.

251

WHAT is the right way to treat a Christmas-flowering cyclamen when it finishes flowering?

Move it to a cool, north-facing window and keep feeding and watering it till it stops making new leaves, which will be in June. Then dry it off. Re-pot it in August but keep it cool till plenty of flower buds are showing.

252

WHY has my tradescantia changed from pale green leaves with white stripes, to plain dark green leaves?

Since the striped leaves are more attractive, you should promptly snap off any shoot with plain leaves. Give the plant maximum light (but not direct sun) and it will win back its stripes. The reversion to plain green leaves begins through lack of light. But the shoots with plain leaves seem stronger than the others and if you leave them on they will soon give you a plant with no striped leaves at all.

253

WHY do some of the leaves of my tradescantia develop brown, dead patches? If it is a disease, what is the cure?

This is an easy plant, but it likes good light, and no direct sun. It also wants ample water without being too wet. The browning is not a disease and is most probably due to erratic watering. Given the right light conditions and careful watering it should get over the trouble.

254

WHAT causes Christmas Cactus to flower in April and never at Christmas? It is perfectly healthy in appearance.

The Christmas Cactus has a twin called Easter Cactus and few people know them apart. Yours is almost certainly the Easter Cactus, Rhipsalidopsis rosea. The Christmas Cactus is Schlumbergera truncata.

255

HOW can I prevent the lower leaves of my rubberplant (Ficus elastica decora) from dropping off and leaving a long bare stem. Several friends have had the same experience? What is the cause?

There are several possible factors – erratic watering, temperature variations, and so on – but the main trouble is our poor winter light, and it is difficult to prevent. The only way is by ensuring good light and by skilful watering. It is better just to accept this failure and cut the plant down to less than one-foot tall in April, so that it can start again.

256

WHAT can one do with a rubber plant when it gets so tall as to be touching the ceiling? Can it be cut down without killing it, and if so when should this be done?

If you want to keep it going on, you can train it along the picture rail. Alternatively, cut it down to less than one foot in April. Put powdered charcoal on the cut till liquid rubber stops oozing out. It will probably produce several new shoots and you can either grow it as a multi-stemmed plant or select one stem and trim off the others before they make significant growth.

257

HOW can one persuade a poinsettia to produce those lovely scarlet bracts? I have been told to keep the plant away from artificial light till the red develops, but this does not seem to work.

From mid-September to Christmas (or till the red bracts appear) cover the plant with a cardboard box from 6 o'clock each evening till 8 each morning. In other words, give it complete darkness for 14 hours out of the 24 for that part of the year.

258

WHEN should a Swiss Cheese Plant (monstera deliciosa), which is nearly four years old, be repotted? What compost is best?

Give it a size larger pot in April, using a rich compost such as John Innes No. 3. Keep on repotting every year at that season using a size larger pot each year till it reaches a 12-inch (30 cm) pot. After that, careful and regular feeding will keep it going for three or four more years, by which time it may need replacing. Frequent weak doses of plant food (such as Phostrogen) should be given, but never strong doses.

259

WHY does my Swiss Cheese Plant, which is three feet tall, make plain, heart-shaped leaves instead of the normal divided leaves with wide fingers?

It is normal for the first three or four leaves to be plain, but where it happens on a mature stem it suggests that the plant needs much more light (though not direct sun). So, to be on the safe side I should see that the plant is placed where it can get all the light it requires. But I should think the absence of cut leaves probably indicates nothing more than immaturity.

260

WHAT is the correct way to cultivate Cyperus alternifolius? It is watered carefully and is healthy, but I am told that it would be happier standing in water, which seems to be strictly against the rules.

You are right about the rules, but this plant does not conform to them. It is sometimes called the Umbrella Plant, and likes to stand in a shallow saucer of water. If you do not give the roots these wet conditions, you may find the leaves going brown at the tips despite constant care. It also likes warmth and shade.

· 261

HOW should one treat an Avocado Pear plant, grown from a stone, when it gets too big for the house? Can it be planted outdoors? Failing that, can it be reduced in height?

The Avocado Pear (Persea gratissima) is not hardy enough to survive our winter outdoors. Cutting it down to less than a foot tall in April may solve the problem. Since in nature this plant would grow to 60 feet (nearly 20 metres) tall, it has a limited life as a pot plant. It should be replaced by a fresh seedling inside 10 years.

262

WHAT can one do with a Mother-in-Law's Tongue which has become pot-bound? I should like to split it.

Who wouldn't. The answer is to repot it in May. Sanseviera (Mother-in-Law's Tongue) makes a number of rooted sucker shoots, which crowd the pot. When re-potting, pull off all these rooted suckers and pot them separately.

263

WHERE can I get seed or plants of those dwarf varieties of chrysanthemum sold as pot plants?

They are not *dwarf varities – but standard varieties which have been dwarfed by manipulation of day-length. This process involves a sequence of artificial light and black-out so that the plants are induced to flower before they reach natural height. If you take cuttings from these and grow them in the normal way they will make tall plants.*

Chapter Five

Lawns

264

WHY does a new lawn go bumpy a few weeks after the grass gets going? Should it be levelled off by rolling? And, if so, when is the best time?

There are two reasons for the unevenness of the surface. First, there may be pockets of soil settling where it was not made sufficiently firm beneath the surface. Next, some of the grass roots tend to push up a few tiny mounds. These mounds can be firmed down by rolling, when the ground is not too wet, at any time. But general levelling should not be attempted by rolling or it will make the soil too compact. Hollow spots should be corrected by the addition of a little sifted soil. Bumps that are too bad can be corrected by lifting a square of turf, removing a little soil, and replacing the turf.

265

HOW long should one let the grass grow for a quality lawn?

All the year round I suppose! Height of cut depends on the purpose of lawn. If you want it to look like a tennis court, cut it down to three-sixteenths of an inch. But a good decorative garden lawn is easier to maintain if the mower is set for a half-inch cut all through the summer and ¾-inch in winter. A play lawn can be a little longer – ¾-inch in summer and an inch in winter.

266

WOULD a lawn of chamomile save the labour of mowing? and would it stand normal wear?

It would not stand much traffic but it would save on mowing. Chamomile is decorative and fragrant especially when walked over gently. It would be rather expensive and slow. It takes nearly 2,000 plants, each to be put in separately, for a lawn of 200 sq. feet – quite a small lawn – because the plants need to be set out four inches apart each way. Weeds would soon pop up in the spaces between plants and weeding must be done by hand – not with weed-killers. So really, it is a bit of a luxury idea.

267

HOW effective are growth regulators on lawns? Would they help avoid the situation where the grass gets too long while the ground is too wet for the mower?

Growth regulators are all right for lawn edges to save trimming, but not for the whole lawn. The treatment would be expensive and the results patchy. If the mower wheels or roller are skidding, mowing must wait till the ground dries, but a Flymo airborne rotary mower works in all conditions, so the problem never arises.

268

HOW sound is the advice that using a grass-box when mowing would get rid of weeds? My lawn is mown regularly, but the clippings are left on the surface and it has been suggested that this is why the lawn is full of weeds.

Mowing kills off annual weeds anyway. Seeds borne on the wind will continue to invade the lawn no matter what policy is followed regarding mowing. However, when weeds are in flower on the lawn it is worth using a grass-box on the mower to avoid scattering large quantities of seed. While this will not get rid of the weed problem, it will at least reduce it so that less lawn weedkiller will be needed.

269

WHAT is the best practice to adopt regarding worms in a lawn? Worms are said to be good for the soil. If so, is it better to leave them? Or since their casts tend to damage the lawn, should they be got rid of? And since the birds eat worms, is it dangerous to use wormkillers and so poison our feathered friends?

Worms do the soil good, but their casts damage the grass. So, while encouraging worms in the rest of the garden we should try to get rid of them from the lawn. Wormkillers will not endanger birds, provided the right wormkiller is used and that it is properly applied. A chlordane wormkiller applied as a liquid will work below the surface and no dead worms will come up for the birds to take. Treatment can be given at any time when wormcasts are seen, but for a routine annual treatment choose September, before the worms start burrowing down deep to escape winter cold.

270

WHEN patches of lawn go brownish, and rough and some of the grass dies, does this indicate fusarium disease? If so, why does the trouble keep coming even after approved fungicides have been applied?

The symptoms described, especially patches dying, suggest that the roots are being eaten by leatherjackets (grubs of the Daddy Longlegs). It is worth treating affected patches with a soil pest killer such as bromophos or diazinon.

271

WHAT causes a mysterious little heap to appear on the lawn sometimes in summer? It is too small a heap for a mole-hill, too dry for a wormcast, and there are no signs of ants, so it cannot be an anthill. Whatever it is, it seems to attract the occasional bee.

The bee is the clue. The heap sounds like the work of the Solitary Bee. Unlike all other bees, this one is a loner and she makes her little nest in the ground, throwing out soil as she does it. Provided you note the spot and don't sit on it, there is no need to do anything about it because the bee will do you no harm. If needs must, you can puff a little derris dust into the entrance hole.

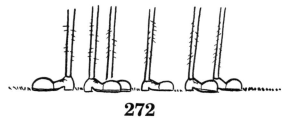

272

WILL Daddy Longlegs do any damage to a lawn?

The cranefly (Daddy Longlegs) itself does no damage but it lays eggs which hatch into a serious lawn pest – the leatherjacket. This pest, the larva of the cranefly, eats the roots of the grass and by the time it is detected the damaged root of grass is dead or dying. There is not much that can be done to the fly when it is laying its eggs in summer, but watch must be kept in spring for small brown patches appearing in the lawn. If the browned grass can be pulled away easily, it has almost certainly lost its roots and the lawn should be treated with bromophos, H.C.H. or other soil pesticide.

273

WHAT is the best way to get rid of moles in a lawn?

There is no best way and no easy way. Trapping requires considerable skill and a thorough knowledge of the moles' runs. The problem with other methods, such as gassing, is that moles move great distances and by the time the molehills are found the creatures are too far away. You can get these little smoke generators (for some reason, called "fuses") from garden chemists. Some people use (as bait) worms that have been dipped in poison. Others drop castor oil seeds into the run. But the worm is the best clue: that is what the mole is seeking when he burrows under the lawn. So, if wormkillers are applied regularly enough to clear out the worms under the lawn the moles will turn elsewhere. I give no guarantee but it has worked for me.

274

HOW can one prevent a bitch from wetting the lawn? Or failing that, what is the best way to cope with the brown patches left behind?

There is absolutely no substitute for training the animal to go elsewhere. There are several brands of deterrents but they need frequent renewal because they are not long lasting, and while they can be reasonably effective in protecting a pet plant, it is not so easy to protect a whole area of lawn. Training and proper exercising, I repeat, are the answer. Where the wetting is spotted immediately, a prompt and thorough hosing down will minimise the effect. So will the application of soda water, but it is a bit much to expect the bitch's owner to be stalking her with a soda syphon at the ready.

275

WHEN should lawn mowing be resumed after the winter rest?

First of all, there need not be a complete rest from mowing during the winter. In any dry, frost-free spell the mower (at its winter cutting height) can be given an airing. But regular mowing should resume as soon as the rate of growth justifies it – which will depend mainly on the weather. As a rough guide, try weekly mowing (at the winter setting) from mid-March. As soon as possible you should reset the mower to the summer cutting height and then mow twice weekly if possible.

276

WHAT is the remedy for patches of coarse, flat-growing grass which the lawn mower skates over?

The grass is called Yorkshire Fog, and should be attacked with an old knife. Slash the roots in all directions with the knife, especially just before mowing. Keep repeating the treatment before each mow. If the trouble is too bad, you can uproot the offending grass and put down a sprinkling of fresh soil with lawn seed in it.

277

WHY do some small patches of grass go to seed when less than two inches tall? I am told that this grass is called poa annua and should be got rid of. If so, why? and how can it be done?

Poa annua is the Annual Meadow Grass and is unpopular in lawns because it seeds so freely (especially on acid soils) to the detriment of better perennial grasses, and can leave bare patches in winter. To get rid of it, you must mow twice a week, with the grass-box on and take away the mowings complete with the meadow-grass seeds. Since this grass is an annual, it will disappear if it is thus prevented from re-seeding itself. Feeding the lawn also will help by stimulating growth in the perennial grasses.

278

WHAT causes the unsightly pattern known as Fairy Ring on an otherwise perfect lawn? And how can these rings be blotted out?

The trouble is a fungus which spreads in an ever-widening circle, like ripples from a pebble dropped in a pool. The fungus can be very stubborn, and difficult to eradicate. Epsom salts at two ounces to the gallon (one gallon to 10 sq. yds) sometimes works. Where that fails, try sulphate of iron at one ounce to a gallon of water. If all that is ineffective the answer is to change the soil.

279

WHERE bulbs are planted in a lawn, does this harm the grass? Does it create difficulties over matters such as feeding, mowing, and control of weeds?

Obviously it is easier to maintain a lawn with no bulbs growing in it, but it would be absurd to suggest that bulbs do any harm in the lawn. Indeed, most people would agree that they are well worth the extra trouble they create over such jobs as mowing. They are no problem regarding lawn feeding. And the weeding programme can be adjusted to avoid harming the bulbs with a weedkiller. Generally, I should say that where a perfect, picture lawn is required, bulbs could make the job difficult. Perhaps the best answer is to have one lawn with bulbs and one without.

280

HOW much soil should be sprinkled over grass seed when sowing a new lawn?

Extra soil is not needed. The seed should be scattered evenly, and then the soil should be raked in all directions till almost all the seed disappears. Then the ground should be firmed gently with the back of the rake. Seed these days is treated with a bird deterrent, so there is no danger of seed loss through bird activity. The small percentage left uncovered by the raking procedure is not important.

281

WHAT should be done about a newly-sown lawn which comes up all weeds? Weedkillers apparently must not be used on grass till it is some months old.

That is correct for normal lawn weedkillers. But firstly, most of the weeds coming up in a new lawn are annuals and will be killed by regular mowing. If too many remain, after the first 3 or 4 mowings, use a special weedkiller called Actrilawn which is prescribed for young grass.

282

HOW does the special sand called "Lawn Sand" revive grass and kill weeds? Where can I get this special sand?

Lawn sand is not simply sand but a mixture of sand and chemicals. You can make your own by mixing three pounds of sulphate of ammonia with one pound of sulphate of iron and 20 pounds of sand. This mix is used at four ounces to the square yard, and is applied in dry weather. The sand is used merely to make enough bulk to aid an accurate spread of the chemicals since these have to be used at a low dosage rate. The iron kills weeds and the ammonia feeds the grasses.

283

WHAT can be done to control a tough lawn weed (I don't know its name but it is not clover) which survives 2-4D lawn weedkiller applied at double strength?

These weedkillers should NEVER be applied at anything stronger than the prescribed dose. A double-strength dose would knock out the leaves before they could take in enough to kill the roots; so would do little good. The weed is probably speedwell. Mecoprop or fenoprop are the best lawn weedkillers for this and other small-leaved weeds. These two are incorporated in several general lawn weed-killers.

284

WILL sulphate of ammonia act as a weedkiller on big lawn weeds, plantain and dandelion for instance? I know that sulphate of ammonia is basically a fertilizer.

Yes, it sometimes works. Put a large pinch in the heart of the weed and it will shrivel up within a short time.

285

WHAT is the advantage of using a combined lawn food and weed-killer instead of giving separate treatments for feeding and weeding?

Using the mixture saves work provided it is applied at the right time. But few weeds can be tackled effectively in early spring, while some don't come through till May. So it would be wasteful to apply the stuff too soon. Judgment must be used to decide whether the lawn needs feeding or weeding or both. And unless both are needed at the same time, it is better to use one or the other alone. Also, in the weed-and-feed combinations some are specifically for autumn use and some for other times. So careful choice should be made.

286

WHEN mowing a lawn, with a mower which incorporates a roller, a dark-and-light striped effect is produced, which is said to be detrimental to the grass because it indicates flattening or crushing. For that reason, one is advised to vary the direction of cut. How often, and in what way, should the direction be varied?

There is no serious ill-effect unless mowing is done in precisely the same "lanes" in the same directions for some time. Nevertheless, the best and simplest rule is to change directions every mow. If one mow is done on east-west and west-east lines, the next mow should go at right angles, that is north-south and south-north. It helps if, after a few weeks, the lines are switched to the diagonals.

287

WHICH part of the day is best for mowing? – morning when the dew is still on the grass or evening when it is dry?

Neither time is ideal. For much of the year, the time of day does not much matter, but in hot sunny weather good timing is a help. Early morning is the best time, while the grass is still turgid and upstanding rather than evening when it is limp. Limp grass does not stand up to the blades. But the mower should not be used while the grass is covered with a heavy dew. Mow as soon as the dew goes off. And you can hurry it off by swishing the grass thoroughly with a long thin cane.

288

WHICH is the better tool to use for keeping lawn edges tidy, shears or edging knife?

Each has its specific uses, but I think the general rule should be to trim with the shears. The half-moon edging knife should be used only occasionally, because it tends to remove a bit of lawn. What is more important, is that these tools should be used at the correct angle. Too many people tend to make perpendicular cuts. The edging knife at this angle leaves an upright edge which MUST crumble. Whichever tool is being used, it should lie back at an angle of about 45 degress. With the knife, this gives an edge which should stay firm for some time. With the shears, the angled cut gives a tapered finish to the grass at the edge and encourages neat growth.

289

WHY do we use two different types of lawn fertilizer, one for spring and the other for autumn?

There are several mixtures, not just two, based on the seasonal and other factors. The main point is that while nitrogen is essential in spring, because we want to stimulate and sustain growth throughout the summer, it would be wrong to overdo nitrogen in autumn. It would encourage young growth, which would be rather soft to face the winter. Hence we vary the basic nitrogen-potassium balance according to the season.

Chapter Six

General

290

WHAT type of plants are the Frankincense and Myrrh in the Christmas Story of the Wise Men?

They are not strictly plants, but gum resins (used as incense) from trees which do not grow in our climate. Frankincense comes from a Browallis, and Myrrh from a Commiphora, whose resin was also called Balm of Gilead. The plant sometimes called Myrrh in our gardens is a herb called Sweet Cicely, which tastes like aniseed.

291

WHAT can one do with a large heap of stones dug out of some extremely stoney soil? After wheeling countless barrowloads, and using what I needed for making paths, I find my new garden is dominated by a large pile of stones.

You won't like the answer. Wheel them all back, spread them, and dig them in again. It is reasonable to rake the odd bucketful off the surface, but if your soil is naturally stoney you will not improve it by taking the stones away. It is better to put something in. The soil wants manure, peat, leafmould or other bulky and fibrous material. But removing the stones would change the nature of the soil and that is bad practice.

292

WHAT is a root-wrapped plant? and has it any particular merit or purpose?

'Root-wrapped' is another name for 'container-grown'. No-one seems yet to have hit on the ideal name for this class of plant, which embraces all those subjects sold as growing – rather than dormant – plants. For instance, you can buy roses which have been lifted and washed clean of soil. But both the lifting and the re-planting have to be done during the plant's rest period – from mid-autumn to late winter. If you buy a "root-wrapped" rose bush it may be in full bloom and can be planted at any time without disturbing the roots. Garden centres, as they are called, established this practice and they first used pots or tins to hold the roots. Nowadays, black plastic bags have replaced the pots and the term root-wrapped seems to have been adopted.

293

WHY do so many authorities approve the use of secateurs to prune fruit trees and roses (although they must bruise and damage the stems)? Old gardeners always use a pruning knife and despise secateurs.

It takes a good deal of skill (and practice) to use a knife efficiently and not to make a mess of the job, while good secateurs do a perfect job without bruising – and are very easy. So part of the answer is that the average domestic gardener does not get enough practice to use a knife efficiently. But it is also a fact that modern secateurs are well designed and well made and do not harm the plants.

294

HOW dangerous for plants are high temperatures? On hot days I find that the greenhouse can get up to 100°F despite full ventilation, an open door, and shading on the glass.

Quite bad. Moist heat does less harm than dry heat, so it helps if you keep the place damp by frequent hosing of floor, benches, and walls. A pane of glass can be removed at the end opposite the door, to promote an air current. The smaller the greenhouse the greater the temperature problem, because small volumes of air heat up or cool down much quicker than large volumes. Hence more ventilation is needed and the ventilators need more frequent attention.

295

WHICH 'May' is referred to in the proverb: 'Cast ne'er a clout till May be out'? Is it the month or the blossom?

The proverb dates back to early in the 18th century and I know no records to indicate what was meant. But it is generally acknowledged to be a warning of the danger of putting aside warm winter clothing. So unless the seasons were much more predictable than they are now, it is unlikely that the proverb would refer to the month. And if the seasons were predictable there would be no need for the warning given by the proverb. Hence it is more likely to refer to something influenced by the weather – such as the hawthorn (May) blossom. But another distinct possibility is that the author was referring to the arrival of the May Bug, the flying Cockchafer Beetle.

296

HOW do people maintain plants in hanging baskets indoors without either letting the plants dry out or getting drips on the carpets? Do they use step-ladders?

One way of watering is to give water in small quantities regularly so that there are no drips. There are hanging baskets available with saucers built into them so that ample water can be given to ensure that the roots do not dry out and that no surplus drips down. Reaching up to a hanging-basket if it is above head height may need a step-ladder. However, a tip to make watering easier than reaching up with a jug or watering can, is to pop ice-cubes on the surface of the compost. Obviously this will cool the roots, but not enough to do any harm, as the ice will melt slowly.

297

WHEN growing bamboo (such as arundinaria) for the production of staking canes, how long should one expect it to take the canes to grow to a reasonable thickness? Does it help if some of the thinnest ones are removed?

The question suggests a possible mis-conception of the way this subject grows. Canes do not increase in girth during growth and so the drill is to cut each one when it has made a suitable length. Removal of thin canes (or any canes) will help the remaining ones; not because it gives them room to swell (they won't) but rather because the plant will concentrate its energies on the remainder. Greater thickness may be achieved in older plants, but the chief difference is that the older plant will produce a bigger quantity.

298

HOW harmful is ivy on house walls? Is it true that it causes excessive dampness for instance?

Ivy does no harm. I don't know where the tale originates that ivy causes dampness, but it is the opposite of the truth. Ivy is one of the best wall-covering subjects, since it is happy in any type of soil, is evergreen, and climbs without support. It uses short aerial roots to cling to the wall, and its strong leaves shed water rapidly so that the wall beneath is kept dry. Any shoot growing out from the wall should be snipped off and the leading shoots should be pruned when they threaten to go up on to the roof.

299

WHAT is the plant that produces the oil or essence called vanilla which is used as a flavouring in cooking? As vanilla essence is sometimes difficult to obtain and we have to make do with 'vanilla flavouring', I wondered whether I could grow the plant.

The plant is Vanilla planifolia and its seeds are used to produce the essence. The plant is an epiphytic orchid, not difficult as orchids go, but it needs an orchid house with a steamy atmosphere, I think you would need a reasonable knowledge of orchid cultivation, a large hot-house, and a bit of luck. Better make do with buying some vanilla flavouring. Some shops sell vanilla pods.

300

WHAT risk would there be in painting a dead tree stump with creosote? Would this be bad for the soil? Also, regarding sucker shoots coming from the base, could they be treated with creosote?

Creosote can be used if care is taken. If it is applied to the stump and the sucker shoots, and not splashed around, it should not do any harm. Repeated applications will kill the stump, and the same applies to the suckers. If there is risk of getting creosote on the lawn or plants, some plastic sheeting may be needed as protection. Also, if tender-leaved plants are growing near enough, the fumes could have a scorching effect.

301

HOW effective would plastic netting (one-inch mesh) be as a windbreak in a very exposed garden? I am advised that this will keep wind off, but it sounds like trying to hold water in a sieve.

It is better to filter the wind than try to stop it with a solid fence. If you aim a powerful jet of water against a wall or close fence it is liable to bounce over the top at full force or knock down the fence. The same jet of water directed against an open-work fence or netting will filter through and have no damaging force in it when it gets to the other side. The wind behaves in the same way, and Netlon plastic netting will stand the wind and the weather in a way that will help the plants.

302

WHEN taking over a neglected garden with weeds more than head height, should one chop them down with a sickle, or use a weedkiller?

This is definitely not a job for chemical weedkillers in the first place. Cut the weeds, while they are still green if possible, and make a compost heap. It is almost impossible to use weedkillers when wading through tall weeds and it could be dangerous to the operator. You would still have to cut and clear up, anyway, so chemicals would not really save work.

303

WHAT is the origin of the old saying that "One year's seeds mean seven years' weeds"? It cannot be literally true, as seed will either grow or die in that time, so what does it mean?

Surprisingly, there is some literal truth in it. Each year's cultivation brings some weed seeds up to germinate, and leaves some too deep. Research shows that it DOES take seven years before the last of any one year's weed seeds is germinated. I don't know where the saying originated, and I doubt whether the author realised how literally true it was.

304

WOULD salt help to clear the green growth on a smooth cement garden path? This growth turns dangerously slippery.

I would not use salt, because it is nasty stuff to tread on to the lawn or into the house. And it would keep the paths permanently wet. Try a fruit tree tar-oil wash (at normal dilution) or sulphate of iron at four ounces to the gallon to ten square yards. Don't use the tar-oil if you want to keep the path bright and clean. You can get an algicide called Dimanin which is used for cleaning pots and greenhouse glass but the cost may be much too steep for paths.

305

HOW can one rid a garden of thistles? All efforts have failed year after year.

Some will be coming from seed scattered in earlier years and the first essential is to remove and destroy the flowers promptly. There is a country saying that thistles cut in June are cut too soon, but cut in July are sure to die. The plant's root reserves ensure strong re-growth after early cutting down, but these reserves should be exhausted by July. So the remedy is to keep cutting them down (bearing in mind the June-July saying) until they stop coming.

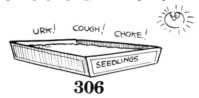

306

WHY do the seedboxes in my greenhouse become covered with green algae which chokes the seedlings? How can this be killed without harm to the seeds?

Light encourages this algae. You should cover seed-trays with glass and brown paper till the seeds are through. As an extra precaution, add Cheshunt Compound when watering seedlings.

307

DESPITE carefully stocking a garden pool with fish, oxygenating plants, and other subjects, the surface is covered with a green moss. How can this be removed without using anything harmful to plants or fish?

It could be that the fish have eaten the oxygenators. However, if this is a mature pool, it ought to be clear unless there is a fault in the pool design, giving too small a volume of water in relation to the surface area: which means too much shallow water, as in a saucer shape. If not, it is just a matter of waiting till the lilies cover enough surface with their leaves to keep the light off; and the oxygenators (perhaps some fresh ones) have got to work. The algae problem often arises with a new pool but usually clears itself when the plants are properly established.

308

WHAT insecticide should I use to get rid of mosquitoes around a garden pool without harming plants and fish?

None. If mosquitoes are a nuisance, the pool must be wrongly stocked. There ought to be some Golden Orfe in it, and these would catch the mosquitoes. Go to a specialist who sells garden pool plants and fish; show him a list of what you have (both plants and fish) and he will tell you whether you are wrongly stocked in any other way besides your lack of Golden Orfe.

309

WHERE normal treatments fail, could a plague of slugs be due to the state of the soil? For some years, I have fought a hopeless battle against them, and I am told this is because my soil is rich in humus due to heavy dressings of stable manure.

That could be the answer. Cut out all bulky manures for two years – and substitute chemical fertilizers. Keep the garden clear of weeds and rubbish which could harbour slugs. Also continue to use slug bait to capture all you can.

310

WHICH is the more effective way of using slug pellets, scattering them all along the row, or placing them in small heaps at intervals?

Put them down in small heaps which can be conveniently covered. Do not scatter them around, or birds may take them and suffer. Cover the heaps with plant-pots (tilted to let slugs crawl under) or anything convenient. Where pets may wander, it is better to use a very heavy stone instead of a pot – something animals cannot knock off to get at the pellets.

311

WHAT harm is there in keeping insecticide for use a day after mixing? Instructions with some say that when mixed as a spray (with water) they must be used the same day, which is a wasteful idea when one wants to spray only a couple of plants.

Some insecticides when diluted or exposed to light or air, will break up and cease to be toxic (to pests as well as humans). Use a small hand-spray to mix only the quantity needed for immediate use. It is wise to keep the concentrate in the dark, by putting the bottle inside a dark container if the bottle is of clear glass, or it may lose its effectiveness.

312

WHAT is the remedy for woodlice, which we call "hardbacks"? We have caught a large number under stones in the rockery, but can't keep them out of the house. No insecticide seems to penetrate their hard shell?

Despite their hard shell, woodlice are vulnerable to insecticides, because they have a soft underbelly. Lindane dust or Sevin dust sprinkled where they run would be effective. They are rather harmless anyway, living largely on dead plant material.

313

WOULD a pressure-type sprayer be suitable for applying lawn weedkiller? I have one complete with hand-lance, which makes light work of other spraying jobs.

It is wiser to use a watering can. A fine spray could drift and kill nearby plants. Besides any container used for weedkiller is best not used for anything else, and that includes the watering can. If you must use the same can for more than one type of job, be careful to wash it out thoroughly.

314

HOW can I make a paraffin insecticide? Is there a formula for mixing paraffin, soft soap and quassia chips?

There are some old paraffin recipes but they involve heat, which is a needless risk when you can do a simple job with medicinal liquid paraffin. Just agitate the liquid paraffin with an equal volume of lime-free water, plus household detergent at about one ounce to five pints. Four ounces of this emulsion, mixed with water makes a gallon of spray.

315

HOW often need a rain-barrel (used for watering plants) be cleaned out to prevent fungus troubles?

At least once a year. Scrub it out with washing soda and if a thick deposit has formed on the inside, disinfect with a two per cent solution of formalin (one pint of 38/40% commercial formaldehyde in six gallons of water). Then rinse thoroughly and air it. The water in the barrel can be kept sweet throughout the year by the use of Condy's Crystals (permanganate of potash) added regularly in just sufficient quantity to keep the water a pale pink.

316

HOW can one stop pigeons eating garden plants – apart from growing the plants under an expensive "fruit cage"?

You can get repellants, such as Morkit, but quick new growth makes protection difficult. There are various bird scarers but whatever type is used the birds seem to ignore them after a while. A narrow strip of Netlon netting stretched over a row of Brussels sprouts – though leaving the plants totally exposed at the sides – seems to frighten the pigeons off.

317

WHAT can be done to protect plants from stray cats? They come into the garden, scratch in the soil and do the plants no good. Is there something which can be used to scare them off?

Scaring is difficult. You can get "Scent-Off Buds", to put around individual plants, but it is important to create conditions the cats will dislike, such as hard, firm soil, coarse cinders, and disinfectant smells. Once a cat uses a part of the garden it will come back regularly unless the smell is promptly killed by something like a strong disinfectant.

318

WHY is it that rainwater is healthier than tap-water for plants?

It is NOT healthier, especially if it comes via the roof and guttering because it can pick up harmful bacteria, on its way down. For plants which dislike lime (azaelas, for instance), the rain water is certainly better than tap water but care should be taken to keep the water clean. The barrel should be covered, and some permanganate of potash (just enough to make the water a pale pink) should be put in the water.

319

WHAT use is farmyard manure when it is nearly all straw? I understand that straw is bad for the nitrogen in the soil.

Straw consumes nitrogen as it rots, so if it is put straight into the ground it may not do any immediate good. But it will later release the nitrogen back into the soil. There will be plenty of nitrogen in farmyard manure, and the manure should be heaped up to rot before being spread or dug in.

320

WHAT is the brown furry caterpillar with pretty markings which is said to be poisonous to the touch?

The caterpillar of the Brown-tail moth can cause a nasty rash if handled. But it can hardly be considered a menace. The remedy is to spray fenitrothion on plants where the pest is suspected of being active.

321

WHAT is the method of preparing common borax for use as a remedy for ants?

There is an old-fashioned ant bait made by mixing powdered borax and castor sugar in equal quantities. The mixture can be placed where the ants run, or small heaps can be set down near their nests. The bait should be covered to keep it dry.

322

HOW dangerous is creosote to plants. Can it be applied to a wooden fence around the garden?

Creosote must not get on to a plant or the effect would be fatal. Even without touching, its fumes are harmful and scorching. In winter, it could be used to treat a garden fence without risk. It should not be used in a greenhouse.

323

WHAT is the bug that can be used to kill greenhouse whitefly? And will this bug itself do any damage?

There is a little parasite called Encarsia Formosa, which destroys whitefly. Write to the Royal Horticultural Society at Wisley, Woking, Surrey for details of how to obtain the parasite. The method is to place the parasite on an infected plant, where it will lay its eggs in the whitefly larva. The egg hatches into a grub which eats the pest. It is important to realise that the right conditions (constant warmth) need to be maintained to keep the parasite happy, and this may be difficult in the average all-purpose domestic greenhouse.

324

HOW should one treat seaweed collected from the beach, to make it into good compost?

Spread it thinly and leave it for a couple of days at least to drain well. Then mix it thoroughly with straw or garden waste. Finally stack it like any other compost heap and leave it till the heap is reasonably crumbly.

325

WHY are we told that it is no use saving seed from F1 hybrid? I saved some from an F1 hybrid tomato and produced some lovely plants from the seed.

An F1 is cross-bred from two distinct varieties. You certainly CAN save seed from an F1 plant but the plants from such seed will NOT be the same as the hybrid parent. Their fruits could be better or could be worse. It is a gamble. To produce F1 seeds, the two parents MUST be cross-pollinated each time – which, incidentally makes the seed dearer to produce than "straight" seed from a single variety.

326

HOW is it that birds eat poison berries? It seems a dirty trick by Nature to make poison berries such as Yew so tempting. I have seen birds poison themselves, or at least I have seen them take the berries.

Birds will swallow the berry and digest the flesh (which is NOT poisonous). But the poison pip (unbroken) passes straight through and is deposited in their droppings. If you chew yew you may be poisoned. But birds don't chew yew stones.

327

WHAT is the best way to get rid of a plague of earwigs, apart from trapping them, which makes me shudder?

It depends where they are. There are plenty of sprays to clear them off plants. Or you can try making a bait. Mix four ounces of Lindex insecticide in a quarter-pint of water and stir in two teaspoonfuls of golden syrup. Stir all into half a pound of oatmeal. Small heaps of this bait, covered with upturned boxes, should then be placed around plants needing protection, or where the pests are known to run.

328

WILL seeds left over from one year be fit for use in the following year?

Most seeds will be viable if they have been stored dry and cool, but sow extra, to allow for a percentage of failure. Onion and parsley seeds do NOT keep well. Where there is doubt, a sample should be tested. Take ten seeds from a packet and place them inside a folded piece of damp blotting-paper inside a flat tin (such as a throat-pastille tin). Close the tin and put it in the airing cupboard. Check it daily. Whatever percentage germinates, can be taken as the percentage viability. In other words, if only seven grow out of every ten, you must sow ten for every seven plants you want.

329

WHY are we told not to mix certain simple fertilizer chemicals? One of my books gives a fertilizer formula which includes nitrate of soda and superphosphate, but another book says these two chemicals should not be mixed. Why not?

You can mix them for immediate use in soil or composts, and there is absolutely no danger. But if you mix more than you want to use straight away, they will re-act on one another while in store. This puts nobody in danger and it does no harm, but it reduces the nutrient value of the nitrate of soda.

330

WHAT is "sharp sand"? I tried to buy some to mix my own potting compost but was offered builders' sand. Is that sharp?

Builders' sand, if salt-free, can be used in some peat mixes for seeds and plants but it is too "soft" for a John Innes mix. "Sharp" in this context means coarse and gritty.

331

WILL the dust and grit swept up with leaves in the road make the leaves unsuitable for the compost heap?

Dust and grit do not matter, so the sweepings could still be good material. But it might be better to keep road sweepings separated from other garden waste, in case there is any tarred gravel or oily debris among them. They should be all right after a few months of weathering.

332

WHAT is chitted seed and what is its particular merit?

Seed that has been made to start sprouting before sowing, is called "chitted". Some cucumber seed, for instance can be difficult to germinate, and seedsmen offer it ready germinated ("chitted"). Cyclamen is another popular subject available as chitted seed. There is an extra charge for the chitting but it eliminates the risk of germination failure.

333

WHAT causes pelleted seed to fail sometimes when ordinary seed germinates all right? Is it poor quality seed, or is the pelleting material faulty?

Neither. But if the seed-bed or boxes are allowed to go dry, pelleted seed will fail. No seed should be allowed to dry out after sowing, but this is infinitely more critical with pelleted seed. The coating must remain nicely moist till the seed inside germinates. In other words, slightly more moist conditions should be aimed at to make certain there is no drying out of the coating during the germination period.

334

WHY is it that carefully-sown seeds so often fail, while in the wild they seem to come up 100 per cent? Is it because garden conditions do not properly match nature?

It is a big mistake to think that Nature gets 100 per cent germination. Nature is recklessly extravagant in scattering seeds in the wild, and the failure is much worse than in cultivation. Scientists reckon there are up to half a million weed seeds in every square metre of fertile ground in the wild. That is a clue to Nature's over-provision.

335

HOW does John Innes Potting compost No. 1 differ from Numbers 2 and 3? Sometimes I am advised to use No. 2 and my garden centre offers only No. 1 and tell me it does not matter.

The three potting composts are basically the same formula, namely 7 parts (by volume) medium loam, 3 parts peat and 2 parts coarse sand. The difference is in the nutrient element. For No. 1 mix, you add to each bushel three quarters of an ounce of carbonate of lime and four ounces of the John Innes fertilizer. For No. 2 mix you double the lime and fertilizer; and for No. 3 mix you treble them. John Innes fertilizer is available from garden shops. Its formula is 2 parts (by weight) superphosphate, 2 parts hoof and horn meal, and one part sulphate of potash.

336

WHAT is the special quality of the loam in John Innes composts? I understand it comes from stacks of old turf so I stacked some when I dug up the lawn to grow vegetables.

The ideal loam for John Innes composts is that from stacks of turf taken from clay ground. The turf should also have a strong root system, as the root fibres are an important part of the loam. And it ought to be sterilized before use.

337

HOW can one prevent 'damping-off' fungus killing seedlings? Home mixed John Innes seed compost gives good results with some seeds but damping off attacks the odd box of seedlings. Sterilizing has been suggested but how can this be done in a small greenhouse?

The loam (soil) ingredient in John Innes composts ought to be sterilized. This is difficult to do at home on a full scale. But small quantities of soil can be sterilized in the oven – enough to mix as much John Innes compost as is needed for three or four seed-boxes. And, of course, the operation can be repeated if more boxes have to be sown. The drill is to leave the loam spread on a shallow tray in the oven for one hour at 150°C. Another method is to put some loam in a plastic bag and treat it with formaldehyde. Dilute the chemical as directed on the tin and pour into a plastic sack containing the soil. Secure the neck of the sack and leave it sealed for three days. The loam must then be exposed to the air for a month before being used. A further precaution with seedlings is to water them with Cheshunt compound solution to prevent damping off.

338

HOW useful are tea leaves and tea dregs on the garden?

They do some good and no harm, warm or cold, with or without sugar and milk. Tea is a drink made from dried leaves and so is nitrogenous, making it an acceptable plant food, slightly acid (tannin). Tea leaves can be put on the compost heap for tidiness, or around plants if lightly hoed in so as not to look untidy.

339

WHAT is the best way to use spent hops from the brewery? What dosage should be applied for vegetable growing?

Don't confuse spent hops with hop manure, which is reinforced with fertilizers. Spent hops are good, like leaf mould, for improving the soil texture, and can be dug in generously, but a general fertilizer should be used in addition as the spent hops are not at all rich in nutrients.

340

HOW much would salt in the soil affect the flavour of a crop, if for instance a fertilizer made from seaweed, were dug into a bed for the growing of tomatoes? Presumably seaweed might be salty so would the tomatoes taste salty?

If the use of a seaweed fertilizer could make a crop taste salty, mushrooms would have an awful flavour! Anyway plants don't like soil with more than one thousandth part salt in it.

341

HOW can chimney soot be used on the garden? And has it any fertilizer value?

It yields a little nitrogen but had better not come into contact with plants till it has been exposed to the weather for about three months. It can also be used – fresh or weathered – on the soil around the base of a plant to deter pests, such as slugs.

342

HOW long should it take to make a heavy clay into a workable soil? My soil has been turned over to a full spade's depth every year for six years but the clay is as solid as when I started ten years ago. What more can I do?

The precise time is not predictable but inverting solid clay every year may not work. That way, you bury the surface two inches of live soil and it is inclined to go dead. Either keep the soil SAME WAY UP or dig shallowly. A shallow surface layer of workable soil is created after only one season. If you avoid inversion you can increase the depth of that layer by an inch or so each year. Adding fibrous material (such as leaf mould) or gritty sand helps break down the clay. So does gypsum (calcium sulphate) which can be forked in at up to half a pound to the square yard.

343

WILL one fertilizer do for all crops in the kitchen garden? And can I mix my own?

Ideally each crop wants separate treatment. But you don't go far wrong with vegetables if you use a balanced general fertilizer mixture such as 5 lbs sulphate of ammonia, 7 lbs superphosphate, 1 lb bonemeal and 2 lbs sulphate of potash. This mixture can be used at four ounces to the square yard.

344

HOW much risk is there in putting a thick layer of strawy stable manure around the trunks of ornamental trees? I am told it could rot the trunks.

Not unless it is too fresh, but it should NOT go close to the trunks at all. The main roots are like outstretched arms, with feeding roots near the outer end, under the tips of the branches. So plant foods intended to feed a tree should be put in a circle approximating to the tree's extreme reach.

345

WOULD a heavy dressing of farmyard manure on the greenhouse border be the cause of blackening and shrivelling of pot plants on the shelves? If so, what would be wrong with the manure?

It could be if it was absolutely fresh. Manure in that state might give off a large amount of ammonia gas, and this could scorch the plants in an enclosed atmosphere. In any event, farmyard manure is better stacked outdoors to ferment for a few months before use.

346

WHAT is green manure and where can one get it? At what rate should it be applied?

Green manuring means raising a fast-growing, leafy crop, such as mustard, and digging it in live. There are special seed mixtures available to sow for green manuring. As to rate of application, well it is just a matter of digging in the whole lot where it stands. It adds fibre — the way leaf mould would do — to the soil.

347

WHAT particular merit is there in the rule that gardens should be given manure in the autumn and lime in the spring? (Or is it the other way around?) Sometimes the ground in autumn gets too sticky before I can do much digging. The problem then is whether to manure or lime when doing the spring digging.

First of all the rule, which can be applied either way, is merely a rough-and-ready formula for keeping lime and manure well apart from each other. When mixed, the lime re-acts on the nitrogen in the manure, turning it into ammonia gas which then escapes. All that is necessary is that manures or any nitrogenous fertilizers should not be applied within six weeks before or after an application of lime. Lime is not needed every year, anyway. Perhaps one third of the vegetable garden should be limed each year. So the rule does not really create many complications. If in spring you find that the ground has had no autumn treatment, better apply fertilizers and forget the lime. Incidentally bulky manures (as distinct from fertilizers) are better applied in autumn so that they can rot down and let the ground settle before spring sowings or plantings.

348

WHY are bonfires banned in some areas? Is their ash of any value for the garden? I believe in former times many gardens had bonfires smouldering permanently and they made lovely soil.

The general objection to bonfires is that smoke is in every way bad in the atmosphere. The slow-burning bonfire of old was extremely bad because its incomplete combustion created harmful fumes. Garden waste should be put on the compost heap unless it is too tough to rot. Woody waste and bones should be put into a quick-burning incinerator. Although bones would rot slowly in the soil, the danger is that they would encourage vermin.

349

WOULD a seed propagator be any help in a heated greenhouse? If so, would it be costly to run?

Winter woollies are not superfluous, just because you have an overcoat. There are plenty of times when freshly-sown seed wants a higher temperature than is needed for the greenhouse, and that is where the propagator can create the micro-climate needed by the seeds.

350

WHEN the soil has hardly any worms, is it any good for sowing and planting? Can worms be imported to improve the soil?

Worms go deep in cold weather, so don't be deceived when digging in winter. They also have a sense of humus, so dig in leafmould and other bulky stuff to encourage them. Meanwhile, the soil will crop reasonably if fed properly. Importing worms is like putting the cart before the horse. Worms don't make bad soil good; but they make a good soil better. If you dig in stable manure or garden compost to make the soil good the worms will come. But if you put worms into bad soil – particularly soil short of humus – they are more likely to die than to multiply.

351

WHEN a garden is all clay, so hard one cannot get a spade into it, what can one grow on it?

Tired, of course! It should be turned over when rain makes it just moist enough but not sticky. In the autumn, fork in gypsum up to half a pound a square yard, and leave it rough. By the following spring it should grow almost anything.

352

HOW can one quickly transform a garden on shallow, hungry soil into a blaze of bright colour?

It is easier than it sounds. A hungry soil obviously needs feeding, but a minimum of such feeding – a general fertilizer about a couple of weeks before sowing – is enough to accommodate annuals. Annuals, both hardy and half-hardy, flourish on poor soil. On rich ground they would be liable to make leaf and stem at the expense of bloom. Hardies can be sown direct into the ground but half-hardies want the protection of a frame or greenhouse to get started in April, for planting out when spring frosts have finished. Easy hardy annuals include calendula, clarkia, godetia, larkspur, love-lies-bleeding, and love-in-a-mist.